TWO HOMES

*A Parent's
Guide to*
*Joint Custody
in Canada*

TWO HOMES

A Parent's Guide to Joint Custody in Canada

LAURIE COULTER

A Lorraine Greey Book
HarperCollins*Publishers*Ltd Toronto

To the reader: This book does not presume to take the place of proper legal counsel. No action should be based solely on the information in this book, and the publisher and author take no responsibility for readers' actions.

Canadian Cataloguing in Publication Data

Coulter, Laurie, 1951–
    Two homes : a parent's guide to joint custody in Canada

ISBN 0-00-637625-8

1. Joint custody of children — Canada.
I. Title.

HQ777.5.C68 1990   306.89'0971   C90-094173-1

Published by
HarperCollins *PublishersLtd*
Suite 2900, Hazelton Lanes
55 Avenue Road
Toronto, Ontario
M5R 3L2 Canada

Produced for HarperCollins*PublishersLtd* by
Lorraine Greey Publications Limited
Suite 303, 56 The Esplanade
Toronto, Ontario
M5E 1A7 Canada

Design by Holly Fisher & Associates

Printed in Canada

For Mark and Alyssa.

Contents

The three stages of the divorce process. Aiming for an amicable divorce. Choosing a parenting plan that is right for your family. Options that are open to you: sole custody, split custody, divided custody, joint custody. The impact of divorce on children.

Motivations for choosing shared parenting. Developing a positive relationship with your former partner. Assessing the suitability of a shared parenting plan for your child. Where will you live? Shared parenting and your career.

Steps you can take to make your journey through the legal maze less stressful. Finding a lawyer with a cooperative approach. Keeping your legal costs down. Mediation as a method of resolving issues between separating couples.

Who are the best candidates for mediation? Working out a separation agreement. Avoiding a contested divorce. How to obtain an uncontested divorce with and without a lawyer. Changing a shared parenting plan.

Sharing the financial responsibility for your child. Negotiating the financial arrangements in a separation agreement. Spousal support. Division of family property, including residential or recreational property, possessions and pensions. Financial odds and ends: wills, credit cards, car insurance, moving expenses. Changing the financial arrangements in your agreement. Tax concerns. What to do when support payments are not made. Dealing with financial inequalities between the two homes.

The advantages and disadvantages of one parent's staying in the family home. Moving to a new home and helping your child feel comfortable there. Taking belongings from home to home. Coping with stress during the adjustment period. Where to find professional help for your child or yourself. Developing a parenting partnership. Guidelines for coparents. Alleviating problems on holidays and special occasions. Long-distance parenting. Building a life as a single person.

Breaking the news to your child. How to help your child overcome her fears. Setting up a new home for your preschooler. Easing transitions from one home to the other. Ways to help your child understand when he will see each parent. Common pitfalls for parents to avoid. Day care. Starting school and choosing a kindergarten teacher. When your child is ill. Special considerations for infants and toddlers.

Breaking the news to your child. Helping your child adapt to the separation. Loyalty conflicts and reunification fantasies. How to tell if behavior is related to age rather than to the divorce. Setting up a home for a schoolchild. Maintaining different rules in different houses. Children who look after themselves. What you can do to help your child at school. The importance of friends and activities.

Breaking the news to your teenager. Reactions during the adjustment period. A teen's concerns. Parenting plans for this age group. Striking a balance between schoolwork, chores and activities. Age-appropriate behavior of adolescents. Seeking professional help. Changing time-sharing arrangements.

Grandparents and former in-laws. Dating and repartnering. Questions to consider before remarriage or cohabitation. The effects of one parent's remarriage on the parenting partnership. Stepparenting when both partners have children or when one partner is childless. Helping your child adjust to a stepparent and stepsiblings.

A Word from the Author

T he first time I heard my son give his two addresses in response to a friend's question, "Where do you live?", I felt a mixture of relief at the ease with which he answered and a gnawing doubt as all the old questions flooded my mind. Had his father and I made the right decision in choosing a shared parenting plan after our marriage ended? Was Mark going to be all right next year, the year after? What lay ahead for our family?

David and I knew one divorced couple who shared the parenting of their children, but we had lost touch. The books on the topic all seemed to discuss joint custody from either a very positive or a very negative viewpoint. What I wished for when we were making our decision was a parent's guide to help us decide what was best for our son. We needed to hear the voices of mothers and fathers who were actually living shared parenting.

I hope this book answers that need. Every generation's parents have learned from one another. They have shared their dreams for their children, their fears, their successes and their failures. This book is written in that spirit: the spirit of sharing information, parent to parent. Just as the end of your marriage is the beginning of a new life for your family, *Two Homes* is a starting point in helping you plan that new life. And for those who have already chosen shared parenting, I hope it will provide some options and information on issues that may surface in the years ahead.

A note on the language used in this book. The language describing families that have undergone the process of separation and divorce is an evolving one. Terms coined by the legal profession are being replaced by family counselors with words that are felt to more accurately and sensitively reflect the changes in the makeup of families. For example, some counselors have replaced the term "joint custody" with "shared parenting" or, sometimes, "coparenting." Because both the legal profession and governments still use the term "joint custody," I have used it here in the legal sense to refer to a parenting plan in which both parents make decisions regarding major issues affecting their child, such as health, education or religious upbringing. In "joint custody" the actual "physical custody" of the child may range from one parent taking on the responsibility of the day-to-day care of the child to both parents sharing that responsibility. It is in the latter sense that I have used "shared parenting" and "coparenting" in this book. Although much of the information in *Two Homes* is about shared parenting, it can be applied to any type of parenting plan.

Many people have helped me in my new life and in the writing of this book. I would particularly like to thank the parents and children I interviewed for sharing their lives with me. They welcomed me into their homes, were patient as I struggled with a sometimes balky tape recorder and answered my questions with amazing openness. Their practical advice and reflections on their experiences form the heart of this book. All their names have been changed to preserve their privacy.

I would like to thank Carole Curtis, Rhonda Freeman,

Josef Rich, Joyce Kelly and Winnie Larsen for their professional insight; lawyer Sandra Meyrick for her helpful comments on the manuscript; my publisher, Lorraine Greey, and her managing editor, Shelagh Wallace, for their helpful comments and never-ending optimism; my editor and new friend, Meg Taylor, for her courage in working with a book-editor-turned-writer; my old friend Robyn Magee for her faith in me; and, last but not least, my wonderful family.

L.C.

Beginning a New Life

1

The first three or four days after he left I wasn't really functioning at all. I remember sitting for long periods of time just staring out the window. Finally Catherine said to me, "Mommy, aren't you ever going to get out of that chair?" It was only then I realized I had to deal with my children. I couldn't sit there anymore.

After a marriage ends, it takes time for the couple to join the world again as individuals. We grapple with sometimes overwhelming emotional upheaval, both within ourselves and in our relationships, especially with our children. At this time of crisis, we may drift through the days accompanied by a sense of unreality, a feeling that this is not the way it was supposed to be.

Mental health professionals have divided the emotional process of marital separation into three stages. The first is the most difficult to endure. During this period, the foundations of the marriage are collapsing, leaving two very frightened people and often one or more small witnesses. Children are sometimes stunned to find themselves faced with parents who are like two strangers, acting in an uncharacteristic and frightening manner.

The negative emotional feelings experienced by many divorcing parents include denial, rage, depression and remorse—all felt at an intense level. This emotional roller coaster begins with the disintegration of the couple's relationship and continues through the decision to separate and the actual separation. Depending on the circumstances of the marriage breakdown and the personalities of the partners, the aftereffects of this stage can last for a few months to a year or two after the separation.

In addition to trying to deal with the reactions to the end of the marriage within the immediate family, each partner must also cope at this stage with the reactions of the extended family, friends and acquaintances. The seemingly simple task of telling people can be stressful, because our society hasn't devised ways to announce a divorce or guidelines on how to respond to such news. I remember carrying boxes out of the house on the day I was moving. An older neighbor was backing her car out of the driveway. Because she wasn't a close friend, I had forgotten to tell her of David's and my decision, and when she came alongside she gaily called out, "You look like you're leaving home!" The poor woman was mortified when I told her that, yes, in a way I was.

Like a death in the family, news of a divorce may evoke reactions ranging from embarrassment to dismay to sympathy. Unlike death, divorce may bring disapproval rather than support. Depending upon the significance of the relationship to the divorcing person, a person's sense of self-worth may be damaged by disapproval. A lack of support may also increase feelings of loneliness and despair. Happily, the intense emotions felt during this period do diminish in time, allowing the healing process to begin for the entire family.

In the second stage of the divorce process, there is

a growing acceptance of the separation, a sense that it is time to get on with the business of living. Little forays are made into unknown territory, some successfully, some unsuccessfully. New friends are made, a new activity started, a new relationship begun. Old friends and family members who may have disapproved of the divorce have now at least accepted it. The family is still in flux, but the separation of the couple on various levels — emotionally, physically, economically, legally, sexually — is near to completion. Because this is such a complicated, confusing process, and because partners are seldom in agreement about the decision to separate, they are unlikely to proceed through each level at the same rate. This, in turn, can cause further misunderstandings and problems that must be worked out.

In the final stage, the family has truly divided into two functioning units, each headed by a parent. The grieving over the death of the marriage has ended and the former partners have adjusted to their new status. New routines and ways of living have been established, bringing with them a sense of emotional security.

AIMING FOR AN AMICABLE DIVORCE

Every time he got scared or I got scared and we treated each other differently from how we had always treated each other, we upset the other person. It just got to be a horrible, horrible situation, which was not good for the kids and not good for us. If we just treat each other as we've always treated each other, then we can at least function.

An "amicable divorce" may appear to be a contradiction in terms. Divorces are supposed to be "messy." And, in fact, they are messy from stage one right through to stage three, but that doesn't mean we all have to engage in lengthy divorce battles. There are alternatives.

For some, finding those alternatives may require assistance. During the early stages of a divorce, there seem to be an overwhelming number of emotional and practical problems to solve. A good counselor, whether that person is a mental health professional, a social worker or a minister or rabbi, may be able to help. Initially, a couple may want to explore saving their marriage; however, if they later decide to separate, a counselor can assist them in dealing with the negative feelings that accompany divorce. Feelings of blame and a need for revenge, for example, can poison a couple's ongoing relationship as parents. Acknowledging that, in most cases, both partners share responsibility in the breakdown of the marriage is a first step in preparing for a life apart. A counselor will also help a couple see that they aren't failures and that their children won't be failures because the marriage has ended. Sometimes the solution to great distress *is* separation, and there is honor and respect in that.

Nevertheless, many parents wonder if they should try to keep their marriage together "for the sake of the children." This is a highly personal decision, with many factors to be weighed. Researchers have found that a family in which the children live in one home with both parents provides the best climate for the psychological growth of a child; however, this ceases to be the case when hostile parents create an atmosphere of tension and conflict. A family in which the parents have divorced, that functions well and in which the child has access to both parents provides a healthier climate than a family marked by parental strife.

After deciding to end the marriage, some couples separate within a few weeks. Others live together for a while in the same house, sleeping in separate rooms, until they can make other living arrangements. Still others begin drawing up a formal separation agreement, sometimes called an interim separation agreement, while others prefer to wait before starting legal proceedings. Whatever the case, a parenting plan should be worked out as soon as possible even if it is considered a temporary arrangement.

PARENTING PLANS

It is an unfortunate fact of life that during times of great stress we must sometimes make the most important decisions of our lives. Choosing a parenting plan after a marriage ends is one of those times.

When you are ending a marriage, it is often difficult to put aside feelings of bitterness, anger, sadness, or guilt to focus on the needs of your child. Try to consider your youngster's need to be parented in the way that is best for him rather than your own need to parent in a certain way. There is a difference. What we often take to be best for our child is in reality what is best for us, what we can cope with, what makes us feel good. Unfortunately, when parents become self-absorbed in this way, a child is sometimes seen as the prize awarded to the parent who "wins" the "custody battle." The child's needs are frequently placed second to the needs of his parents.

Rather than treating their child as an extension of themselves, parents need to see him as an individual in his own right. The parenting plan that is developed should be the one that best suits his personality and needs. An easygoing child may be able to cope with, and adjust to, a variety of parenting plans. A child who initially objects to change but eventually comes around may also adjust well

19

to a variety of plans if given enough forewarning and encouragement. A child who is temperamental and wary of new situations may need a plan that has a lot of stability built into it.

By focusing on their child's needs and talking as parents, a couple not only helps their child, but also their own transition from a marriage relationship to a parenting relationship. However, deciding upon a parenting plan takes a good deal of rational discussion, which may not be possible when emotions are running high. Although focusing on your child instead of yourselves is the key, if you find that anger and bitterness are preventing you from communicating, this may be another time to seek professional advice.

In the past when a marriage ended there were few choices to consider. Today there is a wide range of parenting plans available to you. Research evidence does not point to one being more beneficial for all children than another.

The plan you eventually choose is something that only you and your former partner can decide. It is unfair to ask a child to make this decision. Most children have difficulty deciding who to live with, especially in their younger years. They're afraid that, by choosing one parent, they will alienate the other, perhaps forever. After one eight-year-old was asked by a judge which parent he wanted to live with, he turned to his social worker and said sadly that he didn't think he should have to make that kind of decision. Most childcare professionals would agree.

The parenting plans that follow will give you an idea of the options that are open to you.

SOLE CUSTODY
Sole custody, the parenting plan of approximately eighty-five percent of divorced couples in Canada, was chosen by

Anne and Rick for their eight-year-old daughter, Sara. After ten years of marriage, Anne and Rick's life together had become a series of repetitious spats, often centering on what Anne saw as her husband's inadequacies as a father and mate. They had long since stopped loving each other and were now to the stage at which they were happiest when the other was absent. After a visit to a marriage counselor, where they both admitted to being apathetic about saving the marriage, they decided to separate.

Both parents agreed to a sole custody arrangement. Under federal and provincial legislation regarding custody and access, Anne must exercise her rights and responsibilities as the custodial parent with Sara's best interests in mind. Rick's access to their child includes the right to spend time with Sara and to make inquiries and be given information regarding her health, education and welfare. The day-to-day care of Sara is Anne's sole responsibility. Rick writes Anne a cheque each month for child support and spends time with Sara every other weekend from Friday evening until Sunday evening, one evening during the week and two weeks during the summer.

This couple cannot imagine another plan working for them. Their marriage had been traditional in the sense that Anne had stayed home to care for Sara. Rick had often worked late at the office, and although he had helped with the childcare when asked and available, he had taken his lead from Anne. Neither would have found an arrangement that involved more childcare on Rick's part feasible or desirable. This doesn't mean they don't have some problems with the life they've chosen. Anne has returned to the work force but is finding it tough to make ends meet. Rick misses his daughter and she misses him — their evenings during the week are rushed, and on the weekends they no sooner get settled into a routine than it is time for Sara to leave. On the plus side, after a rocky first year for their family, Anne has found a support group of single friends, Rick is becoming more confident in his parenting skills and more relaxed with his daughter, and Sara is doing well.

In this family, both parents have ensured that the father has maintained his ties with his daughter. Rick phones frequently, rarely misses a weekday evening and has never missed a weekend. Anne doesn't discourage her daughter from talking on the phone to her father or spending other days with him that aren't specified in their separation agreement. With this type of cooperation, it is unlikely that Sara will ever find herself in the large group of children who rarely, if ever, see their nonresident parent.

Rick and Anne's parenting plan gives Rick "reasonable access" to his daughter. Access in other sole custody arrangements can range from "no access" for cases in which a child's safety is endangered by the noncustodial parent, to "limited access," meaning that permission must be given by the custodial parent for the noncustodial parent to see the child, to "conditional access" meaning the noncustodial parent must meet certain conditions before he or she can see the child.

SPLIT CUSTODY
In this plan, each parent has sole custody of one or more siblings. Split custody is uncommon in Canada. Parents rarely choose this option and courts rarely order it, believing that siblings are better off kept together. Adolescents, however, may choose to stay with the parent they feel most comfortable with, and this may result in siblings being parted.

DIVIDED, OR ALTERNATING, CUSTODY
In some families, the children live for an extended period of time, usually one year, with each parent. This occurs

mainly when the parents live hundreds of kilometers apart. The parent who has the child living with him or her has total responsibility for childcare, while the other has the right to spend time with the child. For example, the school year might be spent with one parent and the vacation with the other. The courts have tended to disapprove of this parenting plan and parents seldom choose it.

JOINT CUSTODY

In general, joint custody means that the parents share the major decision making regarding their child; there is, however, no statutory definition of this parenting plan in either the provincial legislation or the federal Divorce Act. The act simply says, "The court may make an order under this section granting custody of, or access to, any or all children of the marriage to any one or more persons." Basically, it is whatever people want it to be. Nor are there any official government figures on the number of Canadian families who have joint custody arrangements. The number has increased in recent years, as it has become a better-known parenting option after divorce, but is still very small compared with sole custody.

In one form of joint custody, the decision making is shared, but not necessarily the physical care of the child. Sally and Paul have chosen this plan for their two sons and a daughter, aged seven, nine and twelve. As a self-employed engineering consultant, Paul is frequently out of town on business, sometimes for one or two months at a time. His absences from home proved to be a strain on their marriage and a deciding factor in the type of parenting plan they chose after agreeing to separate. The children's principal residence is with Sally, and their father pays child support. Because of Paul's schedule, the children's time with him has not been specified in their separation agreement. The two former spouses live within a block of each other and the children visit Paul on weekends, at lunch or after school. If he's in town, he meets one child who has a paper route in the morning, helps him with his route and then goes jogging with him. When he's away, he writes and phones his children often.

Sally describes herself as a "living day to day" type of person. The lack of any type of schedule regarding her children's time with their father doesn't bother her, and she and Paul haven't had any major problems agreeing on health, education or religious issues affecting the children. Both are active in their community and feel that the neighborhood and their neighbors have helped provide support and consistency in the children's lives.

Variations of this type of parenting plan include one parent's having the children every other weekend and overnight once during the week, one parent's having the children every weekend, or a flexible time-sharing plan such as the one Sally and Paul follow. In a family I know, the father takes care of the children three weekends of the month and, because his former partner must be at work early, he comes to her home each morning, feeds the children breakfast and takes them to school.

The length of time that the father (in most cases) spends with his children in these types of joint custody arrangements may be the same or slightly longer than that spent by noncustodial parents in sole custody arrangements. This type of parenting plan raises two questions for the primary caregiver, however. Are you willing to share the decision making about your child with a former partner who is unable or unwilling to take on a significant share of the day-to-day care of the child? And will you be adequately compensated for that care? Some lawyers caution that if you call this arrangement joint custody rather than sole custody with liberal access, you may have trouble obtaining an appropriate amount of child support as the custodial parent.

In shared parenting, the daily care and responsibility for the child is shared between the parents. People often assume that this means the child spends an equal amount of time with each parent, but this is not always the case. Nor is the time-sharing plan originally agreed upon necessarily adhered to throughout the child's life. A shared parenting plan must be made with the understanding that the child's needs or the parents' needs may change in the future, and the plan along with them. Several different arrangements might be tried before settling on one that works best for all members of the family.

"Complicated" and "complex" are words that many coparents use to describe their life-styles. Coordinating a child's activities, school holidays, day care, the purchase of clothing and school supplies, and the hundreds of other details involved in a two-homes plan requires a high level of organization, cooperation and commitment. In choosing this plan, many coparents feel like pioneers. They have no relevant childhood experiences to draw on and know few people who have made similar parenting arrangements after a marital breakdown. The parenting plans they devise, by themselves or with the help of a counselor, mediator or lawyer, are tailor-made for their families; however, they do tend to fall into the following categories.

One Week On, One Week Off

Ten years ago, against the advice of family and friends, Gwen and John decided to share the responsibility of caring for their two young children. Both had been hands-on parents and wanted to continue their parenting relationship. They each agreed to look after the children on a weekly basis with Monday as the changeover day. The parent who had had the children for the week dropped them off at school on Monday morning and the other parent picked them up from after-school day care. The children had a set of clothing at each home and other childcare expenses were divided according to salary. When the children were older, they requested a longer period of time with each parent and the plan was changed to two-week periods.

This weekly plan seems to be the most popular arrangement for school-age children. In some families with two children, one child goes to his or her second home one day and the other child goes the next day so that each child has a special night alone with each parent. Sometimes parents take their children out for dinner or lunch midweek on their "off-weeks." While some people find it difficult to change from a family-oriented life-style one week to a single life-style the next, others enjoy the freedom it gives to pursue other interests outside work and family and the enthusiasm they bring to parenting after a week away from their child.

Day by Day

In a variation of this plan, one parent looks after the child during the day, the other at night, and the weekends are alternated. Because I have worked at home since Mark was born, this was the plan that David and I decided upon when we separated. It meant that Mark, who was three at the time, would still spend time with each of us every weekday and would not need to adjust to day care as well as the separation. Now that he is in school full-time, he also spends from Thursday morning until Monday evening with me every other week so that we have a block of unbroken time together. When asked about the time-sharing arrangement we have, he will say that his mom takes care of him during the day while his dad works and his dad looks after him at night while his mom works.

Other time-sharing plans include splitting the week from Saturday afternoon until Wednesday morning or two days on, two days off. Although the day-by-day plan is often used to care for preschoolers, Ed and his former wife, Lydia, have looked after their children in this way for five years since their children were four and eight:

The most common criticism of the day-by-day routine is that it's disruptive for the children, but we haven't found that. They're with me Monday and Tuesday, with Lydia Wednesday and Thursday, with me Friday, and we flip Saturdays and Sundays. There is a lot of back and forthing, but it works. Because of the way I schedule work, they're here for lunch and after school. This is, in a way, their home base during the day. Built into that is total flexibility for whatever events are going on in their lives or our lives, so there's no "They're with me tonight. You can't have them." Absolutely none of that, and I think that's essential.

Parents Move In and Out

Some coparents feel that the stability of living in the same home is good for children after a separation. It gives their children the message that during an anxious time their parents are working together to make life less difficult for them. This arrangement is called "birdnesting" by family counselors. Unless parents are committed to birdnesting, counselors generally agree that having both parents care for their children is more important than having the same physical surroundings. Children may, in fact, find it more difficult to adjust to living in the same home with two different sets of rules than living in two homes with different rules.

On a practical level, birdnesting prevents the parents from separating their finances and assets, such as furniture and appliances. Paying the mortgage on a house and renting two apartments can be very expensive. Some parents rent one apartment to be used by both parents on off weeks. Others stay with friends when they aren't looking after their children, but this is a stressful solution. Add new partners and birdnesting becomes an even more complicated arrangement. For these reasons, it can be a difficult plan to continue for any length of time.

THE IMPACT OF DIVORCE ON CHILDREN

My seven-year-old's self-esteem seems to have gone. She's always saying she's not well. She has a sore throat. She can't do this. She can't do that. Her eight-year-old sister is fine. She's very secure in herself, very loving. The whole world could crumble and she'd survive.

As a newly separated parent, you may worry about the effect the divorce and the parenting plan you choose will have on your child. You may find yourself vaguely remembering statistics about children from "broken" homes or a story half-listened to years ago about someone's child who got into trouble and the teller's knowing look as she said, "Of course, his parents were divorced." A kind of panic sometimes sets in and, instead of dealing with the problems of today, you may find yourself worrying about problems that you think may occur ten years down the road.

There have been many studies on the effects of divorce on children. Like the custody option you choose, much depends on your child and the type of family life you have had and will have in the future. In a study of children's adjustment in joint and sole custody families published in *Developmental Psychology*, researcher Marsha Kline and her colleagues found that ". . . custody and access arrangements are only one consideration in a complex chain of factors that affect child adjustment. What seems to matter for children who have a fair amount of access to both parents is not the legal title conferred on the family, the quantity of access, or the amount of movement between homes but, as we might expect, the quality of family functioning during divorce." In general, the better the parents have adjusted to the divorce, the better the child will adjust.

Like their parents, children also pass through the stages of divorce, experiencing denial, anxiety, anger, grief, sadness and, in time, acceptance, if allowed to heal in a climate of reassurance and love. This process can take a year or more. The intensity and duration of the emotions felt during this period vary from child to child. There is no way to predict how your own child will react. Some children have very minor reactions, although the majority are clearly distressed.

With school-age children, academic performance and behavior at school can suffer during the adjustment period after the separation. Children under stress may be easily distracted, aggressive or withdrawn in class, and their parents may find that, as single parents, they don't have as much time available to help with homework. Unfortunately, children of divorce have sometimes been unfairly labeled as school problems because of what is often a temporary condition as families adjust to their new lives.

Some people believe that children of divorce are more likely to become juvenile delinquents. Studies do seem to show that antisocial behavior can be a problem directly after a separation as children adjust and parental discipline falters under the stress of the early stages of divorce. Nevertheless, long-term problems are more likely to be a result of persistent conflict in the home or poor parent-child relationships rather than the particular family structure.

A positive outcome of divorce for children is the more androgynous role models that their parents provide. Mothers may become more assertive and independent while fathers may become more nurturing.

He's a good kid. The other day I was sitting on the couch and Matt came over and the next thing I knew he was stretched out with his head in my lap. I thought, "This kid's almost fifteen. A fifteen-year-old boy doesn't put his head on his father's lap!" But he wasn't at all self-conscious about it. I loved it of course. As big and gangling as he is, there's a naturalness about him. And it seems he's surrounded by boys who are all wonderful people. They don't seem to need to be stridently male.

As you go through the painful process of divorce, it is important to remember that children are resilient. If parents try to put the past behind them, cooperate on developing a parenting plan that suits their child's needs, and carry out that plan in a positive way, their child will be given the opportunity to heal.

Will Shared Parenting Work for You?

2

I'm astounded at how petty people can be and how much they can let their children be hurt in order to exercise their own resentfulness. People seem to be a little less like that in shared parenting. Maybe it takes a different type of person to agree to go into it in the first place.

In shared parenting, both parents want to be actively involved in raising their children. They want to be there for the scrapes and bruises, the school gossip, the excitement of each new accomplishment, the day-to-day adventures of a child. They believe strongly that their son or daughter will benefit from being cared for on a regular basis by both parents. And they like not having the pressure of raising a child on their own. Not surprisingly, many parents who shared the responsibility for child-rearing in their marriages choose shared parenting after the separation.

Other motivations for choosing this parenting plan are not child-focused. They include a parent's feeling less guilty if the parenting is shared with a "wronged" former partner, or a belief that he or she will have more time for work or social activities. Neither should be primary motivations for choosing coparenting, and in certain cases shared parenting should not even be considered. In an article published in *Social Work*, Meyer Elkin suggests that if any of the following negative factors are present, shared parenting is not suitable for the family:

- Child neglect
- Family violence (physical, emotional or sexual), including child abuse
- A history of addiction in one or both parents
- Mental illness
- Parents who have been unable to agree in the past about the rearing of their children
- Parents who cannot differentiate between their needs and their children's needs
- Families who have been very disorganized in the past
- Children who are unlikely to adapt to joint custody arrangements or who rebel against joint custody
- Families in which both the mother and the father are unalterably opposed to joint custody
- Logistical problems that make a joint custody plan difficult to carry out

Studies have shown that joint custody of any description is least successful when one parent is forced into it. As listed above, there are a number of valid reasons for a parent to be opposed. However, other reasons may stem from a lack of knowledge about shared parenting, or pressure from family, friends or professionals to reject it as a parenting option. Because it is obviously difficult to discuss a parenting plan if only one parent is familiar with all of the options, the parent who is least informed should be given information on the topic. Once both parents are informed, they can decide whether or not the personalities and needs of the family suit shared parenting.

YOUR RELATIONSHIP WITH THE OTHER PARENT

Trusting that your former partner can be a good parent is a necessity. I heard a story about a child who was returned after a two-hour drive and the father had liquor on his breath. I couldn't live with that. I know that, although Steven was a lousy husband, he's a good dad and prides himself on being a good parent.

We have many roles that we play in our families: spouse, lover, parent, friend, son or daughter. In shared parenting after divorce, one ground rule is being able to separate the role of spouse from the role of parent and, in doing so, to accept the end of the marriage partnership but not the parental partnership. In most custody arrangements — except those that protect a parent and child from abuse — your former partner will always be connected to you through your child. In shared parenting that bond is much stronger than in other parenting plans. Because there are more reasons for contact, there are more opportunities to play out the destructive games that can harm a child. For example, shared parenting won't work if one spouse sees the arrangement as an opportunity to reconcile with the other. Or if the parents continue to act out their bitterness each time they meet or talk. This is why the first priority of couples embarking on shared parenting is the setting aside of negative feelings associated with the marital relationship to concentrate on whatever they are negotiating or setting up regarding their child.

Will you be able to do this? Burying the past is never easy. It may help to know that many former couples do establish a positive relationship with each other in time. In a study of divorced parents, sociologist Constance Ahrons found that more than half of them were what she calls "cooperative colleagues" or "perfect pals." Although they still felt some anger over the marriage breakdown, they didn't allow it to interfere with the parenting of their children.

Twelve years after their divorce, Aaron and Jan are now cooperative colleagues. Initially, though, there was a tremendous amount of anger between them, so much so that they were both frightened by it. Because their hostility didn't cloud the fact that they both respected each other as parents, they were able to work out a shared parenting plan. They found that, if they conducted their "royal battles" over the phone, kept their direct contact to a minimum and stuck to the business of child-rearing when they did meet, they could cope. Gradually, as they settled into their new lives and the children grew older, their relationship changed, becoming less formal and more friendly. When Aaron was offered a two-year assignment in another province a few years ago, he stayed at Jan's home on his weekend visits to see their children. Says Jan, "It just seemed to make sense. So much had changed and so much time had gone by. The picture had changed drastically."

To support each other in the role of parent requires mutual trust and communication. Trust is a commodity that is in short supply after a separation. Any fragile pieces that remain can be swept away by an adversarial lawyer or simple ignorance of the intentions of the other parent regarding the children. The rose-tinted glasses of the early years of marriage having disappeared long ago, each partner retreats behind the mirrored glasses of divorce.

To come out from behind those glasses and begin being honest with your spouse about your feelings and your intentions, although painful, is the first step in rebuilding trust. Each partner needs to be reassured that the motivation of the other is not to take the child away from him or her, and in shared parenting each partner must trust that the other is a good parent who is capable of taking care of their child on a daily basis.

Refusing to talk, making frequent derogatory comments to a former partner or communicating through a child guarantees failure. Coparenting a preschooler requires frequent communication between parents simply because of the child's dependency on his parents. There must be some cooperation in decisions regarding sleep times, feeding, toilet training, day care and illnesses. Regardless of the amount of anger between them, most former partners who are not on good terms do eventually find ways to communicate. They formalize their relationship, keep discussions to matters involving the children and maintain a cool distance (see page 98). As researchers Rosemary McKinnon and Judith Wallerstein note in an article published in the *American Journal of Orthopsychiatry*, ". . . parents in conflict in some areas are fully cooperative in others, and even very angry parents may be able to create a conflict-free oasis for the sake of the child."

Developing a positive relationship—friendly or merely cordial—after a marriage ends takes time and effort, but it is possible and is in the best interests of your child.

YOUR CHILD'S NEEDS

One thing I've had to learn—and it's a difficult thing for our generation to learn—is selflessness. Your child comes first and you put up with a lot for his sake.

What all children need is a loving relationship with both parents. Infrequent or no contact with either parent can damage a child's self-image and self-esteem. In shared parenting, a child has the time to develop a close relationship with her mother and father and benefits from knowing that both parents have made a commitment to care for her on a regular basis. However, there are no studies to indicate that all children will be happier in joint custody arrangements or that all children will be happier in sole custody arrangements. The parenting plan is only one factor in many that affect a child's adjustment to divorce.

When assessing the suitability of a shared parenting plan for your child, you might consider the following factors:

- The age of the child: The time-sharing arrangement may vary according to whether the child is very young, school-age or adolescent.
- The flexibility of the child: Judith Wallerstein explains in her book *Second Chances* that this is an important factor in the adjustment of a child to shared parenting, noting, "Children who are relatively calm and easygoing from birth are more likely to adapt well to joint custody arrangements, as they are more likely to adapt to many other changing circumstances. Children who are cranky and irritable from the start and who have trouble mastering simple routines seem to have more trouble with joint custody, as they do with other changes." In families with children who are easygoing and children who are difficult, parents will need to assess the advantages and disadvantages of shared parenting for each child. This may involve a number of trade-offs. For example, if two of the children seem to suit one time-sharing plan and a third doesn't, the importance of the sibling group

to the third child may outweigh her difficulties with changeovers.

- The needs of the child: Children may express preferences that should be taken into account when deciding upon a parenting plan. They may want to spend more time with one parent than with the other, or they may want to stay in the same school or be near friends. If a child seems afraid to spend time with one parent, the reasons for that fear should be determined, by enlisting the help of a counselor if necessary, before coparenting is agreed upon.

WHERE WILL YOU LIVE?

Most counselors agree that the closer the parents live to each other, the more successful the coparenting arrangement will be. It's desirable, although not always possible, for children to remain in the same schools and to maintain the same friendship and neighborhood ties. It also alleviates stress caused by long commutes. In 1981, Howard Irving and Michael Benjamin, the authors of *Family Mediation*, compared the experiences of coparents with that of sole custody parents. In their Shared Parenting Project study, they found that the couples who lived farthest apart were more likely to encounter problems. Those who did live farthest apart and were satisfied with the arrangement had a time-sharing plan with fewer changeovers between the homes than couples who lived in the same neighborhood.

Living in the same neighborhood raises a number of questions to be considered by parents. First, do you really want to stay in the same neighborhood or would you rather start fresh somewhere else? Will it bother you to run into your former partner at the local supermarket or in the park? Will you both be able to afford to live in the same area? (If you live in a neighborhood where a variety of housing exists, this may be possible, but if one of you earns substantially less than the other and you now live in an area that lacks lower-income housing, there may be problems.) And, most important, are you willing to be tied to one area?

This last point requires some crystal ball gazing, at which none of us is very good. Usually the crunch comes when one coparent is offered a job in another community or becomes involved with someone who lives in another area and wants to remain there. It's worth noting that Canadian courts are now considering long-distance moves by one parent disruptive to the regular contact between a child and the other parent and in two Ontario cases have stopped a custodial parent from moving with her children. In an Edmonton case, a mother with a joint custody arrangement with her former husband was unable to move to Ottawa with her sons. She had remarried and accepted a new job. The justice who heard the case decided that maintaining stability in the children's lives was more important than a parental bond and ruled that the boys should remain with their father in Edmonton. Although it's impossible to predict what course your life will take in the future, it is worthwhile to discuss the mobility factor fully with your coparent in advance of making a decision about shared parenting and to have a plan about how conflicts will be resolved.

Because my ex-wife has British citizenship, this raised great fears in me that she might just up and leave, and I would never see my child again. So there was a great deal of trying to figure out what we would do if she decided to move back to England. We came up with a couple of paragraphs that we put in our separation agreement to the effect that the person not moving would have first choice regarding custody, but then after a year or two the other parent would have the right to have our son with him or her for a period of time. I had heard of examples where the child lived with each parent for a year at a time. After five years of shared parenting, the situation has changed. Now I wouldn't feel nearly so threatened. I'd say, "Take the child for three years; I'll see him when he's sixteen." I think that could work out now.

Every parent who has embarked on a shared parenting arrangement has been asked, "Isn't the going back and forth and having two homes confusing for a child?" The people who ask tend to forget that traditional households with stay-at-home moms are not the norm anymore. In the main, today's children are of necessity flexible. In their lives they may have been exposed to various caregivers in various locations. One caregiver or nanny may have been replaced by another. A home day care for preschoolers may have been replaced by a school day-care program. Because Canadians are so mobile, a change of home may have already occurred. The actual physical moving here and there of shared parenting becomes the norm for many children and is not usually the large problem people think it should be. It is no more confusing than having to adjust to seeing one parent only twice a month.

SHARED PARENTING AND YOUR CAREER
Initially, I didn't have a career. I had a job. My children were my first priority and it was very rare that my job got in the way. Now I have a career and it's important to me. I

didn't make a move to establish a career until I felt I could start moving away from the children some. Now my ten-year-old comes home two afternoons a week by bus because I have clients until five o'clock. I've talked to my children about it and they know how important my work is to me. And they both respect the fact that I've made such a big change at this point in my life.

In coparenting, because the parenting is shared, there may be more energy to put into a career as opposed to sole custody, with most of the parenting falling to one parent. Coparents generally try to strike a balance between work and home. On their "off-weeks," they may put more effort into their jobs, but during their times with the children, their careers often come second.

Work-related questions that parents might consider before choosing this parenting plan include:

- If your child is hurt or becomes sick at school during your time-sharing period, how will you manage?
- Are you prepared to turn down a job in another community?
- Will you be able to give up overtime work during your time-sharing period?

Being self-employed or having flexible work schedules can be an advantage, just as shiftwork or a job involving long hours or frequent out-of-town trips can be a disadvantage, although some parents have been able to develop plans that accommodate unusual schedules. A better system of day care in Canada, shorter work hours and better-compensated part-time work could open the doors to more couples considering shared parenting.

We agreed that we would both have custody, but the schedule of how many days we each would have the children was left flexible. For us that was vital because of the kinds of jobs we have. I sometimes have to go out of town, and if I were at those times required to have responsibility for my children, it just would not have worked.

Successfully Negotiating the Legal Maze

3

I had a good lawyer. I spoke to a few people who had been through a separation and asked for recommendations. My lawyer was a very sensible, pragmatic person, not an alarmist. She brought a great perspective to the situation.

We were both naive about what would happen during the legal process. There seems to be a need to get everything down in such precise terms that it actually erodes the goodwill you may have had and somehow institutionalizes your life. I guess in the long run that may have proven necessary, but I think the process can create an inflammatory situation where there may not have been one before.

Every parent's experience with the legal system will differ according to the level of agreement between the two partners, the lawyers chosen, and the complexity of the family situation. However, many coparents would agree that there are no shortcuts to ending a marriage legally and negotiating a parenting plan that will suit both parents and children. They usually remember this part of setting up two homes as a necessary evil and very hard work emotionally. Nevertheless, there are steps you can take to make your journey through the legal maze a little less bewildering and stressful. The comments that follow are intended to provide information about the legal issues surrounding marital separation and divorce, but are not intended to be legal advice. A lawyer should be consulted before any legal action is taken.

The first step is to acquaint yourself with your rights and responsibilities under Canada's laws on separation and divorce. Although a lawyer can help in this regard, being informed places you on a more equal footing with your legal professional and possibly your former partner. Anything you can do to shorten the amount of time that a lawyer must spend educating you will also save you money. One further advantage is that it forces you to gather your thoughts after a separation rather than jumping directly into the legal process. If you or your child is in danger from a former partner, you should see a lawyer as soon as possible; however, if this isn't the case, it is better to enter the legal process in as rational a state of mind as possible in order to avoid making rash decisions.

The responsibility for making laws regarding the family is shared by the federal and provincial governments. As a rule, the federal government makes laws on divorce, and the provinces and territories have jurisdiction over marital separation, the division of matrimonial property, the enforcement of support and custody orders and the procedures to follow when applying for a divorce. To discover what your child's and your rights are prior to divorce, it is a good idea to obtain information on your province's family law act by contacting the Attorney General's Office or the Department of Justice in your province (see Resource List).

You won't find much information on joint custody in the booklets that will be sent to you. In Canada, the Divorce Act (1985) empowers the court to award joint custody but, unlike the laws in some American states, the act does not contain a presumption in favor of it. It simply recognizes that the custody of, or access to, a child may be awarded to one or more persons. Generally, the courts will sanction joint custody but only when both parents consent to it and are willing to cooperate.

After you have become familiar with your rights, typically the next step is to negotiate a separation agreement and find a lawyer. A separation agreement is a domestic contract between a man and a woman who cohabited and are now living separate and apart. In it, the couple agree on their respective rights and obligations regarding such matters as the ownership and division of property, support, the right to direct the education and moral training of their children, the right to custody of and access to their children, and any other matter involved in the settlement of their affairs. Like any contract, it is enforceable in a court of law — although the courts should be used as a last resort when resolving family law disputes, particularly where children are involved. The separation agreement usually includes a provision that it will become the divorce agreement upon divorce. It should be noted, however, that the courts can choose to disregard any provision in a domestic contract which, in the eyes of the court, would not be in the best interests of the child.

Not all coparents negotiate a separation agreement using lawyers. Some simply agree verbally on custody and property arrangements, and others write and sign their own letter of agreement without the help of the legal profession. Deciding together on the terms of an agreement is desirable, because litigation often destroys the ability to cooperate that is necessary in shared parenting; however, not consulting with a lawyer at all may be unwise. Lawyers are able to point out omissions in your agreement that may have serious implications for you or your child in the future. In addition, a domestic contract (or an agreement to amend or rescind a domestic contract) is unenforceable unless it is in writing, signed by the persons to be bound by it, and witnessed. Each partner having legal representation also prevents the possibility of one partner's saying at a later date that he or she didn't understand the nature and consequences of the agreement. And, finally, if one of you will be paying child and/or spousal support, you should be aware that, to be tax deductible, support payments must be paid according to a written separation agreement or court order.

In their study of Canadian coparents, Howard Irving and Michael Benjamin found that a little over half of them had asked their lawyers to help draw up a shared parenting agreement. Commonly, in this situation both or one of the lawyers will draw up the agreement, which then goes back and forth between the lawyers and their clients until a final form is reached. If there is an impasse, a mediator (see page 50) is sometimes used rather than resorting to the courts; going to court can be an expensive, lengthy and emotionally crippling experience for parents and children alike. Parents may also use a mediator earlier in the process to help them draw up an agreement, which is then taken to their respective lawyers. Or parents may draft an agreement themselves, have it couched in legal terms by one of their lawyers and then reviewed by the other's counsel.

FINDING A LAWYER

Hans went to an adversarial lawyer who was an acquaintance of his parents. He was so turned off by what this man recommended that he called me and said, "We've got to talk to each other." Ironically, it was the first breakthrough in our relationship after we separated. Some of the things that he had been told to do—for example, closing down the joint bank accounts immediately—all said, "I don't trust you. You're not the person I used to know." And then you no longer function as the person he used to know. Fortunately Hans told me, instead of just going ahead and doing these things, and we worked out what we would do ourselves.

Although most lawyers prefer to take on a counselor's role when dealing with a separation or divorce, some still prefer to protect their client's interests by adopting an adversarial stance. At this vulnerable time in a person's life, it is sometimes easy to get caught up in the win/lose arguments of this type of lawyer, especially if you have been deeply hurt by your former partner. However, if a couple has agreed to try shared parenting, one or both partners' choosing a high-powered litigator may ruin a fragile parenting partnership before it has the chance to become stronger. One way a lawyer can do this is by telling a client to stop talking to his or her former partner about the separation agreement and custody arrangements, to let the lawyer "handle everything." While this may be appropriate in cases in which a client or child is at potential risk from the other parent, it is clearly not helpful to parents trying to build a shared parenting relationship.

The best way to find a lawyer with a cooperative approach is by referral from a friend or acquaintance who is separated or divorced. Lawyers you know on a business or personal level can also be approached for recommendations. If these two sources aren't available to you, provincial law societies offer referral services or you can look in the Yellow Pages under "Lawyers." You may want to contact several before deciding on one. When you contact a lawyer's office on your list, it is entirely appropriate to ask the kinds of questions listed below:

- How long have you been in practice?

- How much of your practice is devoted to family law? (A lawyer who specializes in family law is a good choice; one who works in a law office specializing in corporate clients may not be.)
- Do you consider joint custody a custody option? Have you handled joint custody cases before? (A lawyer who has had experience in this area or who has drafted a number of domestic contracts might be more valuable to you.)
- Is there a fee for an initial consultation? What is it?

At the initial consultation, after describing your family situation and what you would like the lawyer to do, you might ask the following:

- Can you give me an estimate of the total fees involved? (A lawyer will not be able to provide you with an exact figure until he or she is more familiar with your case, but he or she can tell you the hourly rate and a range for cases similar to yours. You should ask when you can expect to receive an estimate.)
- Is there a retainer fee? (A lawyer must be retained. This involves the client's signing a written agreement to retain the lawyer to act for him or her. An amount of money is often paid to the law firm on account. It isn't an estimate of what the total fees will be, and any amount not used to pay for legal services is returned to you.)
- Will you provide a letter that sets out the terms and factors determining the bill?
- What is the billing procedure? When will I be billed?

After the meeting, ask yourself if you are comfortable with the lawyer and his or her responses to your questions and concerns. Changing a lawyer midway through the separation and divorce process can be stressful and expensive.

Parents who cannot afford to hire a lawyer can apply for legal aid through their provincial legal aid plan. If you qualify, it will pay all or part of your legal costs. You will be given a certificate which will allow you to choose a lawyer who participates in the program. Applications are available from your local legal aid office. For the location of the office nearest you, look under "Legal Aid" in your telephone book.

KEEPING YOUR LEGAL COSTS DOWN

There are a number of ways to keep your legal costs from escalating above the figure that was given to you on your initial visit to the lawyer's office. The first is to avoid using your lawyer as a counselor. Lawyers bill at an hourly rate. The more senior the lawyer, the higher the rate. Young lawyers may bill as much as $100 per hour and more in the larger metropolitan areas. Depending upon the lawyer, every time you phone to pour out a fresh tale of woe, your bill may increase. This doesn't mean that a lawyer won't be sympathetic to your problems, just that his or her skills are in the area of law, not counseling. Family law practitioners are often familiar with healthcare professionals in the community and, if requested, can provide you with a referral.

The second way to keep your legal costs under control is to direct appropriate inquiries regarding your case to the lawyer's employees rather than the lawyer. For example, if you require information regarding the progress of your case or need to provide the lawyer with further information, the lawyer's assistant or secretary can usually help you. A request for information about your bill can be handled by the firm's bookkeeper or the lawyer's secretary. Appointments can be made through the secretary as well.

Being prepared before talking with your lawyer on the phone or in person is another way to save money. Writing down a list of questions or subject areas you want to cover will be helpful for both of you. During your first meeting, your lawyer will want to know the following basic information in addition to the details of your situation:

- Your name, address, date of birth
- Your spouse's name, address, date of birth
- The names and birthdates of your children
- The date and place of your marriage
- The name of your spouse's lawyer

Although financial arrangements cannot be worked out until a parenting plan has been negotiated, your lawyer may also request financial information at this time (see page 67).

The final and best way to keep your legal costs down is to cooperate with your former partner in arriving at solutions to stumbling blocks in negotiating a separation agreement. The more you can do yourselves, the lower your legal costs will be. When this isn't possible and you seem to be heading for a court battle or lengthy legal maneuverings, mediation may be advisable.

MEDIATION

We skirted a nasty court battle by going to mediation. I would go to a counselor beforehand and get all my angry feelings out there. Then I'd be pretty clearheaded at the mediation meeting. Money was the big issue. There was no question about joint custody for either of us. It was simply a matter of working out financial details. What we ended up with financially was adequate for both of us.

Both federal and provincial legislation concerned with family law promotes mediation as a method to resolve issues between separating couples. Mediators do not take the place of lawyers, however. They help couples draw up their own separation agreement, which is then reviewed by the couple's respective lawyers. Even if the mediator is a lawyer, the couple will still need their own lawyers.

Mediation is available through court-based conciliation services, private mediators and social service agencies or community organizations. Some mediators offer what is called "comprehensive mediation," which means that all matters involving the separation are dealt with; other mediators deal only with child custody and access. Because mediation is a relatively new service, it is not regulated by any laws as yet. Standards of practice have been established by a national organization, Family Mediation Canada, but anyone may call himself or herself a family mediator. More than half of the mediators in Canada hold a postgraduate degree, usually in a mental health discipline (social work, psychology, psychiatry), although there are also many lawyers (notaries in Quebec) specializing in family law who act as mediators. The majority do not work full-time as mediators.

A trained mediator will assist in helping each partner focus on the needs of the child. He or she won't choose sides or make choices for the couple. It's important, therefore, to choose a mediator who is objective and who doesn't tend to favor one party over the other. As in the choice of a lawyer, word of mouth is the best way to find a mediator. Your lawyer will also be able to refer you to several mediators for consideration. If you and your former partner can't agree on a mediator, ask your lawyers to make the choice for you.

Who are the best candidates for mediation? Couples who have emotionally separated from each other as marriage partners and have entered into the next stage in the divorce process are ready to begin negotiating a separation agreement. They must be willing at least to give the process a chance and to give and take a little to arrive at solutions. If a couple has only partially separated emotionally and is focusing on the past rather than the present, the mediator may recommend counseling before they begin to negotiate. However, some people's rage prevents them from being able to use the rational, problem-solving techniques necessary in mediation. They may need the court to make decisions for them. There is also some debate as to whether or not mediation is advisable if one spouse has been physically abused by the other or is dominated emotionally and doesn't feel able to express his or her needs freely and openly.

Some mediators see the couple together, some separately, some alternating between the two. As well, children and other family members or significant others are sometimes involved in the mediation process. The number of sessions varies according to the case, although court-based mediation tends to involve fewer sessions. An average would be six to eight sessions to work out the details of a separation agreement.

At the initial meeting with a mediator, you can decide whether or not you trust this person and his or her approach to mediation. The mediator, in turn, will decide if you are suitable candidates. You will be given the choice between closed and open mediation. In open mediation, the mediator may be asked to prepare a report that could be used in court.

The next meeting will help to define the problems you need to solve. You may be asked to sign a contract that outlines the role of the mediator, what the sessions will entail, what information you are expected to provide (for example, full financial disclosure), the cost per hour, the use of outside experts (accountants, professional appraisers, child behavioral specialists) if need be, confidentiality and legal representation. In subsequent meetings you will explore various solutions to problems and negotiate a draft agreement. You are free to stop mediation if you don't feel that it is working or if you feel pressured into making concessions that you don't agree with. After the draft is completed, it is sent to each spouse's lawyer. (In some cases a mediator will send a letter to the lawyers after each meeting, detailing what has been agreed upon. The lawyers, in effect, draft the agreement as the mediation proceeds.) If one of the lawyers discovers that something is missing or is unclear in the draft agreement, mediation can address the issue or the two lawyers can confer to revise the agreement. The completed agreement is signed by the couple, at which point it becomes a legal document. Follow-up sessions are arranged by some mediators to see how the parenting plan is working out.

Mediation fees vary. Court-based services and those offered by social agencies are free or are based on ability to pay. Private mediators generally charge between $80 and $150 per hour. Lawyers acting as mediators may charge more. Payment can be handled in several ways. You and your former partner can split the bill or share the costs according to earning power. Or one person can pay the fees from his or her earnings and then be reimbursed upon the later sale of marital property. Or payment can be made from a joint bank account.

WORKING OUT A SEPARATION AGREEMENT

The separation agreement helped allay some of my ex-wife's fears. For example, she insisted that she have possession of the children's passports. At one level I think she was afraid that I might take the kids abroad. Given at that stage I was much more mobile and wealthier, that kind of thing could have been feasible for me but not for her, so I gave her the passports. It was not something that I needed reassurance on, but she did. The funny thing is that the separation agreement had many specific clauses like that written into it, which we completely forgot about afterwards.

Parents may be tempted to rush through the negotiation of a separation agreement so that they can get on with their lives. However, although no agreement is written in stone, it is wise to take the time to consider whether you and your children can live with the terms of the agreement on a day-to-day basis for a good time to come. Some coparents try out the shared parenting plan they have negotiated before finalizing their agreement or they start with an interim agreement.

That said, there are few restrictions to what you can cover in your agreement. A lawyer or mediator may convince you to dispense with clauses that simply serve to carry on the marital dispute rather than benefit your child. For example, one woman was dissuaded from adding a paragraph that would prohibit her child from being in the company of her former spouse's new partner. Even when clauses that are added to address one partner's fears at the time of separation are included in the final agreement, they are often forgotten as the family settle into their new lives.

Issues that might be considered in the shared parenting portion of a separation agreement include the following:

- A general statement may begin the agreement to the effect that the parents have joint custody of the child (the term will usually be defined) and that the child's best interests will always come first.

- The time-sharing arrangement is usually specified, or there may be a general acknowledgment of a commitment to an equal sharing of time with the child. To cover times when there is a temporary change in the schedule, some parents put in a clause about the substitution of times of equal length. Others who are more conciliatory put in a general clause about the child's spending such other time with each of the parents as they may from time to time agree.

- Parents with preteens sometimes add a clause that says they will discuss changes in the parenting plan at a child's request. Those with younger children may simply acknowledge they will reexamine the parenting arrangement in the future.

- Parents usually agree to confer on all matters affecting the welfare of the child: education, health, religious upbringing, and activities. They agree that each will have access to medical and school records. A clause may be added saying that day-to-day decisions are the responsibility of the parent with whom the child is living. For parents who are in conflict and therefore less likely to be able to work out problems as they arise, a separation agreement may spell out details in each of these areas; for example, who will attend school events and parent/teacher meetings, who will keep track of doctor's and dentist's appointments, etc.

- A method of arbitrating disputes may be written into the agreement.

- Details regarding holidays may be worked out. For Christmas holidays, for instance, some couples specify who has the child for the upcoming Christmas and then alternate holidays from that year on. Summer vacations may be specified by week or month or are left flexible to be decided upon in ample time before the summer. Other holidays may be shared equally.

- Where the child resides now and in the future is a matter that is frequently covered. Some parents state that they will not remove the child from a given area — city, province, country — for more than a specified period of time without the consent of the other. When there is little trust between former partners, there may be the worry that one parent may take the child outside the country, particularly if that partner isn't a Canadian citizen. Clauses are added to address this concern.
- A clause may be added regarding the relationship of each parent with the child. The parents agree to do or say nothing that will harm the relationship of the other parent with their child. They may agree not to place restrictions on the child or coparent's phoning at reasonable times, or writing.

The financial part of the separation agreement cannot be settled until the parenting plan has been negotiated. Once it is, child support and other financial details can be worked out. (See Chapter 4 for information on financial arrangements.)

As you work through the separation agreement, the ability to communicate with your former partner is a definite asset. In the mediation process, communication between the former spouses is obviously essential. In the legal process, most good lawyers also encourage communication, but misunderstandings may be more likely to occur. Because the level of trust at this point in the separation process is typically low, even couples who are quite conciliatory toward each other are often subject to all sorts of doubts about the actions their former partners will take regarding their children and financial matters once they have consulted a lawyer. Part of this has to do with our concept of divorce as a battle between former spouses. There is a fear that, once the legal profession becomes involved, the verbal agreement between the former partners will change. The more you can do to clear up such misunderstandings, the less stressful the legal process of separation and divorce will be.

One way to prevent misunderstandings when lawyers are preparing the separation agreement is to read the agreement carefully after it has been prepared and before it goes to your partner's lawyer; sometimes standard agreements contain clauses that you and your former partner may not have discussed, and these can cause bad feelings. I remember receiving the draft separation agreement drawn up by David's lawyer and being shocked to discover under "Custody" the sentence "The husband and wife have joint custody of the child, *and the child will have his primary residence in the home of the husband.*" Despite the fact that, intellectually, I knew that David's lawyer had very likely routinely added this, on a rather paranoid level I wondered if David had changed his mind about what we had worked out together. When I talked to him about it, he groaned about the oversight and we simply deleted the last part of the sentence.

Before you sign the final agreement, you should again read it carefully. Once it is signed, you are bound by its terms. Each lawyer signs an affadavit stating that the document and its contents were carefully explained to his or her clients.

This book does not contain a sample separation agreement, because everyone's circumstances are different. If you would like to compare examples of various agreements, you could take a look at the following books listed in the Selected Bibliography: *Family Mediation: Theory and Practice of Dispute Resolution* (Irving and Benjamin), *Sharing the Children* (Adler) and *Sharing Parenthood After Divorce* (Ware).

DIVORCE

Four years after the separation, I fell in love. My ex-husband found that very threatening. Up to then our custody arrangement had been flexible. He sued for sole custody and hired this amazingly cutthroat lawyer, at which point I plunged into the abyss. I had to go through psychiatric evaluations because he was claiming I was a nut, and I wasn't entirely sure at that moment that he wasn't right. After eighteen months of legal battles — we never ended up in court — a mediator said to him, "Don't you hear what she is saying? She will never give you sole custody," and he finally listened. Our divorce was very acrimonious, but I think time has improved our relationship. Finding other people and starting new families has also changed our focus. When we talk, we keep it to basic information about our daughter and our shared parenting arrangement.

Under Canada's Divorce Act (1985), obtaining an uncontested divorce is a relatively simple legal procedure when a couple has negotiated a separation agreement or is in agreement on child custody and support and the division of marital property. Contested divorces, on the other hand, can become incredibly complex and may drag on for years, causing financial and emotional hardship for both former partners. Custody disputes pit parent against parent, each trying to prove the other unfit. Because noncompliance with the court-ordered agreement is common, ongoing litigation is also common. The stress of litigation on both parents, coupled with the length of time the matter is unresolved, often damages their child's self-esteem and relationship with his or her parents. In the end, no one emerges as the winner. This is why less than five percent of divorce cases go to trial and why legal and mental health professionals urge parents to negotiate a settlement if possible.

Under the Divorce Act (1985), which replaced the Divorce Act (1968), there is a single ground for divorce called "marriage breakdown." The breakdown of marriage is established by one of the following conditions:

- The spouses have intentionally been living separate and apart at least one year preceding the decision to divorce and are living separate and apart at the commencement of the divorce proceedings;
- Or one of the spouses has committed adultery;
- Or one of the spouses has treated the other with physical or mental cruelty to the extent that it makes their living together intolerable.

If your marriage has ended for either of the last two reasons, and you are asking for a divorce based on these grounds before you have been separated a full year, you must have proof. The majority of couples simply wait a year from the date of separation before proceeding with the divorce.

To begin the divorce process, you must file a petition with the court. Your lawyer will do this for you or you can do it yourselves (see below). If your divorce is uncontested, you can file jointly, or one person can petition for the divorce (the petitioner) and the other be served with the divorce papers (the respondent). In some provinces, an uncontested divorce can be handled by the court on the basis of a written application and supporting documents. It isn't necessary for the couple or their lawyers to appear in court.

In an uncontested divorce, if the judgment is granted according to the draft filed, the court registrar signs and enters the judgment and mails a copy of it to each of the former partners and their lawyers. A one-month appeal period follows, after which a divorce certificate is issued, permanently ending the marriage. Generally, a divorce becomes effective on the thirty-first day after a judge's decision to grant it. If one spouse appeals the decision, the divorce is not final until after the appeal is settled.

DO-IT-YOURSELF DIVORCE

Divorce changes your legal status in a very significant way. For example, if you have not settled the division of your matrimonial property at the time of divorce, in some provinces you may lose your rights to bring a claim for property division or have only a limited amount of time to do so after your divorce is final. It is also more difficult to apply for support after a divorce. You should be aware of the effect these changes will have on your own circumstances before attempting to handle your own divorce.

If you live in Quebec, the Conseil du statut de la femme has published a booklet on obtaining a separation without retaining the services of a lawyer. A couple choosing to make a joint application for separation in Quebec must go to court. This booklet provides models — blank legal forms, in effect — which you can copy and fill in for the court hearing. It also includes practical advice concerning the filing of the documents and the hearing before the judge.

International Self-Counsel Press publishes do-it-yourself divorce guides for Alberta, British Columbia, Manitoba, Ontario and Saskatchewan. For less than $20 you can also order a set of the forms that you will need to file with the divorce court. (These are also available from commercial stationers.) The authors state that the following circumstances must apply if you want to process your own divorce: you must be able to prove marriage breakdown in a straightforward way; if you don't file jointly, you must be able to serve your former partner without undue difficulty (in other words, he or she is not out of the country or avoiding being served the papers); custody of the children or child support is not a contentious issue; and property claims are not a problem. In addition, the guides give this piece of advice: "If you decide to handle your divorce yourself, remember that even with the recent changes to the law and rules [which make it easier to obtain a divorce], obtaining your own divorce still requires a good measure of intelligence, perseverance, and concentration."

The blank forms in such guides can also be used by couples who are drafting their own agreement and then taking it to a lawyer or lawyers for legal advice.

Most people receive their final divorce papers with mixed emotions: sadness, relief, elation. It is a time for reflection, a time for saying good-bye to the past and for greeting the future.

CHANGING PARENTING PLANS

Court orders awarding custody to one parent or to both parents can be changed at a later date if circumstances have changed considerably. Although a judge can alter the original custody order if he or she feels it is in the best interests of the child, judges are usually reluctant to change custody arrangements that are adequate and have become well established.

There are many factors to consider before a parenting plan is changed. The major question to answer is how the change will benefit the child. It may seem rather simplistic to suggest drawing up a list of positives and negatives, but this is a time when you must be very clear in your own mind about what your motives are. Settling old scores with a former partner by demanding a change in custody is not a valid reason to uproot a child. Your child's life has been drastically changed once; you must be sure that a proposed change will be beneficial.

Parents who have a shared parenting plan are less likely to litigate again than their sole custody counterparts. Most make changes in the plan according to the needs of their child. They generally don't bother to change their separation agreements when they do this, because they have reached a level of trust in the parenting relationship that doesn't warrant the expense of involving the legal process. However, there are times when major changes must be made to the plan, which may call for legal advice. Such changes can be necessitated by the illness of a parent, an out-of-town move by one parent, or a child's adverse reactions to the plan.

For various reasons, some children do not do well in a shared parenting plan. Steven and Michelle had gone to counseling with their three-year-old son, Peter. Although both were loving, caring parents who had worked hard at making their shared parenting plan work, Peter was not doing well. Never an easy child, his behavior had become uncontrollable. Their counselor suggested that they alter their plan to give Michelle responsibility for the daily care of Peter with plenty of access for Steven. They altered their separation agreement to indicate that they were going to try the new plan for a year and assess it at the end of that year. After a few months, Peter's behavior improved dramatically. He was a much more contented little boy. For him, at three, shared parenting was not suitable. The door is open, however, for another attempt at a later date if it seems to be in his best interests.

As children become older, they may express a preference to live in one home. It is sometimes hard to differentiate between your child's sincere wish to be based in one home and his reaction to a difficult situation with one parent by expressing the desire to live with the other. If the former, it should be seriously discussed. Many coparents find that shared parenting has allowed them to maintain strong ties with their children. As long as they are able to trust that those ties will continue even if the parenting plan is altered, they will not feel threatened and will be less likely to set up roadblocks against its occurring.

If changes in an agreement are causing difficulties, a mediator can help you and your coparent negotiate the agreement. Once the revised agreement is reviewed by each of your lawyers, you can again petition the court to have the original court order changed and the revised agreement approved.

Money Matters

4

Initially, I felt very strongly that my ex-husband shouldn't pay support, given that ours was a joint custody situation. I thought I should be able to support the kids during the time they were with me. As it happened, because I had a clerical position, I just couldn't afford day care. I was able to manage, though, as long as he paid for that. It was very important to me that he not give me money to support the kids.

When you are negotiating the financial part of a separation agreement, the goal is to try to ensure that there is an equitable sharing of the financial responsibility for caring for your child and an equitable division of marital property. To reach this goal, coparents have devised as many financial arrangements as they have devised time-sharing plans. Some plans are straightforward; others are complex. All set the stage for how the family will function financially in the years to come and must be considered as carefully as the parenting plan.

CHILD SUPPORT

We split the major bills like the music lessons and the snowsuits and the day care, but nevertheless, I have to have a house big enough for me and two kids on a single-parent income. I was overly optimistic about my ability to provide for them without support.

A mother and father are required to support an unmarried child who is a minor or who is enrolled in a full-time program of education (generally, the first three years of postsecondary education) in accordance with need and to the extent that they are capable of doing so. Traditionally, in sole custody arrangements, the parent with responsibility for the daily care of the child has received child support payments from the other parent. In joint custody plans, the equal sharing of the legal responsibility for the child is sometimes extended to the equal sharing of the financial support of the child. In other words, no support payments are made. Phrases such as "The husband and wife agree to be responsible for his and her own expenses and to share equally the expenses of the child" may appear in the financial part of separation agreements. For this plan to be equitable, though, both parents should earn an equal amount of money and have a more or less equal time-sharing plan.

When one parent earns less than the other and/or is taking on more of the day-to-day care of the child, alternative plans should be made. In these situations, child support can be an emotionally charged issue. A woman, although the lower wage earner, may forgo child support because she doesn't want to feel dependent financially on her former spouse. A man may feel that he shouldn't have to pay more of his child's expenses, especially in a shared parenting plan, just because his former wife earns less than he does; he may believe that the fact that she has a lower income has nothing to do with him. The problem in both these cases is that neither understands that child support payments are intended to support the child, not the former partner.

When negotiating the financial arrangements in a separation agreement, especially those related to child support, you will need to have the following information available:

- Income from all sources:
  - salary (including bonuses, overtime and commissions) or fees
  - family allowance
  - unemployment insurance
  - workers' compensation
  - public assistance
  - pension
  - dividends and interest
  - rental income
  - allowances and support from others (this would include support payments from a former marriage)
  - any other income
- Other benefits:
  - nonmonetary benefits, such as insurance or dental plans, paid on your behalf
- Actual expenses for a twelve-month period:
  - housing (rent or mortgage payments, property taxes, water, electricity, heating, telephone, cable TV, home insurance, home repairs and maintenance or condominium maintenance fees, gardening)
  - food, toiletries and other items (groceries, restaurant meals, makeup, shaving supplies, hair appointments, general household supplies, dry cleaning)
  - clothing (for yourself and children)

– transportation (public transit, taxis, car pools, automobile insurance, license fees, car maintenance, gasoline, parking)

– health and medical expenses (doctors, chiropractors and other healthcare providers, if not covered under provincial health insurance programs, dentist or orthodontist, drugs)

– deductions from your income (income tax, Canada Pension Plan, unemployment insurance, employer pension, union or other dues, group insurance, credit union savings or loan)

– miscellaneous expenses (life insurance premiums, tuition fees, entertainment, recreation, vacation, gifts, baby-sitting, day care, children's allowances, children's lessons and activities, support payments, newspapers, books and magazines, alcohol, tobacco, charitable contributions, pet costs)

– loan and credit card payments

– registered retirement savings program (RRSP) payments or other savings plans

The compilation of this information may seem daunting. However, if you do it one step at a time, it will not seem so overwhelming. The best time to complete some of the list is before you actually separate, while the family's financial records are still available to both spouses. If your partner has looked after the finances, this is a good opportunity to become acquainted with the assets of the marriage, general household expenses and child-related expenses. Your goal is to figure out what your monthly expenses will be after you and your child move into your new home. The next step is to figure out roughly what the other parent's monthly expenses will be so that you can negotiate child support based on relative income and expenses. To smooth the second step it makes sense simply to exchange financial information.

In working out how their child will be supported financially after a separation a couple should take the following into consideration:

- The percentage that each parent will contribute toward the support of the child according to income, living expenses and the time-sharing plan.
- The mechanics of payment. Some coparents keep a record of how much they spend on their child monthly and then compare records at a certain time each month to find out who owes what to whom. Others keep a joint bank account for the child's expenses, depositing an equal amount or an amount proportionate to income each month and withdrawing it as needed. Still others decide on a sum for child-related expenses; for example, the parent who has more of the day-to-day responsibility for the care of the child may be paid a monthly child support payment, which is usually indexed to inflation. Support payments are sent by mail, deposited directly to the other parent's bank account or issued as a series of post-dated cheques. To avoid money changing hands in the form of support payments, the higher-income parent will sometimes pay for a large monthly expense, such as day care, directly. Coparents on a more equal financial footing may simply split expenses as they come up—"I'll buy the raincoat. Will you buy the spring jacket?"
- If you will be receiving child support payments, there are several things to keep in mind. The support payments are taxable. Before you agree to a certain sum,

you should figure out what the after-tax amount is and work with that. You will need to save the difference for taxes each year.

- What expenses are covered in the monthly payments.
- When the child support will end (for example, will it end when the child reaches a certain age? completes high school? completes university?).
- How the costs of the child's postsecondary education will be paid. What these costs cover (tuition, residence, supplies, equipment, etc.).
- How dental and medical expenses will be handled. Who has the better supplemental medical, dental and hospitalization benefits at work? (If a child needs braces, how will they be paid for?)
- How a teenager's car insurance will be paid.
- How differences of opinion on the purchase of major items should be resolved. Some parents have simply agreed that if one parent feels strongly about purchasing something and the other parent feels just as strongly about not contributing to its purchase, the first parent should pay for it himself or herself.
- How will unpredictable expenses be handled?
- What happens if one parent dies. Some people take out life insurance with the children as beneficiaries. When one parent is paying child support payments to the other, the payments should be protected by insurance taken out by the paying spouse.

SPOUSAL SUPPORT

In families in which a spouse has been out of the work force caring for children, spousal support (once called alimony) may be necessary until that parent can find employment or be retrained to develop a skill. A woman with an infant at home may also require support until the child is older. Both legally married and common-law spouses are entitled to ask for support based on financial need. The provinces' family laws contain provisions dealing with support for a spouse upon separation. The federal Divorce Act (1985) covers support orders requested after divorce proceedings have begun. Your lawyer or provincial Attorney General's Office or Department of Justice (see Resource List) will be able to give you advice on applying for support.

DIVISION OF PROPERTY

My daughter's father and I had a joint custody car for awhile because neither of us could afford to buy another one. Fortunately, we both live close to public transit, so it wasn't a problem getting to work on the days we didn't have the car. But I'm sure the neighbors thought it was odd.

Provincial family laws provide strict guidelines on the division of family property after a couple separates. What is included in the description "family property" varies across the country. Obviously, the more property and assets a couple owns, the more complicated their separation agreement becomes and the more need they will have of expert financial advice.

Your lawyer will require the following information:

- Assets
  – properties that you own or have an interest in (nature and type of ownership, addresses)
  – a list of general household items and vehicles and boats, etc.
  – savings and savings plans (types of account, RRSPs, pensions, etc.; institutions; account numbers; amounts)

– securities (shares, bonds, debentures, etc.; number; descriptions)

– life and disability insurance (company and policy number; type; owner; beneficiary; face amount; cash surrender value)

– any interest in an unincorporated business such as a partnership

– debts owing to you from business or personal dealings

- Debts

  – a list of your debts (credit card debts, for example), stipulating when these were acquired (i.e., before, during or after marriage)

Couples who own a house or other residential or recreational property have a number of issues to settle. Will one of the parents be staying in the home? If so, who will pay the mortgage interest? Will the mortgage principal, taxes and house insurance be shared during the period or will the parent who remains in the home pay all expenses and receive a credit for them upon its sale? How long will one parent have possession of the home? Under what conditions will the house be sold before this period expires? How will the sale be handled? If one of the parents decides to buy out the other's share in the home or property, the property will need to be appraised. Usually each partner hires an appraiser and the average of the two appraisal prices is taken as the value of the property. These are just some of the areas that must be discussed if you own property. Your lawyer can help you work out the details.

Placing a value on the contents of the house and other possessions can also be a very complicated procedure. Some couples simply take turns deciding who takes what household item or each draws up a list of the items he or she would like. Items that appear on both lists are traded off—"I'd be willing to let you have the collection of pink flamingos in return for the collection of Bob Dylan albums." In their separation agreements, under "Personal Property," they simply acknowledge that they have agreed upon the division of their personal property.

In dividing family possessions, parents sometimes forget that an older child will consider family property his as well as his parents'. He may associate a certain piece of furniture with one parent—the rocking chair with mom, the armchair with dad—and be upset if it is carted away by the other. He may not want his bedroom furniture divided. Unlike his parents, he may *like* the lime-green-and-hot-pink afghan knitted by Aunt Matilda and may not see the separation as a perfect opportunity to toss it out. Photo albums are also important to a child. If your family photos are glued into albums, it's probably a better idea to duplicate the ones that are important to the parent who is leaving rather than hacking apart the books. One woman took her revenge on her former spouse by crossing out his head in every photo he appeared in—it probably felt good at the time, but is a sad sight for a child to have to face looking through a record of his family's life together.

Pensions are assets that must be considered in property valuation upon separation. This includes company or government pensions and RRSPs. You are also entitled to receive a share of your former partner's Canada Pension Plan credits accumulated during the period of the marriage or common-law relationship. Your lawyer will handle this for you or you can obtain details and an application form from a local Canada Pension Plan office. The value of company or government pensions and the tax implications of their transfer may be difficult to assess without the aid of an actuary or accountant, whom your lawyer will retain if necessary.

As well as dividing the family assets, a couple must divide the family debts. Unless the couple has been involved in a business partnership, these do not include the business debts of a spouse. A schedule for the repayment of debts can be worked out. For example, if one of the spouse's parents is owed a sum of money, the couple will agree to repay the debt after the sale of a piece of property or arrange monthly payments over a specified period of time. The separation agreement should state that each spouse will not be responsible for the future debts of the other.

FINANCIAL ODDS AND ENDS

There are a number of financial matters to deal with at the time you are separating that are not necessarily included in the separation agreement:

- Wills — At the time you are discussing your separation agreement with your lawyer, you should ask about drawing up a new will. In addition, you and your coparent may want to consider who your child's guardian would be if, for the sake of argument, you were both killed at a school concert. Guardians considered suitable before the separation may have alienated one of the partners and may no longer be considered ideal.
- Closing joint bank accounts — The balance of joint savings and chequing accounts is divided and each partner opens his or her own accounts.
- Credit cards — If your credit cards are additional or second cards under your former partner's name or if they

are joint cards, you will need to obtain your own cards if you intend to continue using them. A person who hasn't established his or her own credit rating may find it difficult to do so after a separation. The best idea is to meet with your bank manager and explain your circumstances. Point out how long you've dealt with the bank, that the card was used wisely within the marriage and that you would like to establish a credit rating even if that means putting a low limit on the line of credit. Those with primary cards should transfer them into their name alone.

- Car insurance — The spouse who is designated as the principal driver on a car insurance policy will need to make adjustments to his or her policy to remove the other spouse as second driver. The other spouse will need to take out his or her own car insurance.

- Household contents insurance — A parent who is moving into an apartment will need a tenant's policy; a parent who is moving into a house or condominium will need a homeowner's policy.

- Child's bank account in trust — A couple who are separating may no longer be able to afford to put away money (family allowance cheques, for example) for their child's education. A decision must be made on what the money in the account will be used for (buying a child's bedroom furniture for the other home, for example) or how it will be divided, or, if retained, who will handle the account.

- Moving expenses — Should the partner who is leaving be responsible for his or her moving expenses or should they be shared? Landlords may require you to pay the first and last month's rent. Will there be funds available to do this? If money is tight until your assets are divided, can you borrow the money from friends or relatives?

Changing the Financial Arrangements in Your Agreement

According to the Divorce Act (1985), child support orders must recognize that "the spouses have a joint financial obligation to maintain the child; and apportion that obligation between the spouses according to their relative abilities to contribute to the performance of the obligation." A parent who is receiving or paying support and who wants to alter the original support order due to a change in his or her financial situation can seek a variation proceeding. As the applicant, he or she will want to prove that a variation order is necessary to relieve economic hardship due to a change in material circumstances.

Property arrangements (who got Aunt Mavis's silver tea service or the antique trundle bed from Glengarry County) cannot be altered after the divorce is final, unless kept open by mutual agreement.

Tax Concerns

If you are paying child support, your payments are only deductible if they are regular, periodic payments. A one-time lump sum is not deductible, nor is it included in your former partner's income for tax purposes. It is also necessary that payments be made according to a written separation agreement or a court order, a copy of which should be included in your return.

With regard to child tax credits and dependency deductions, Canada's Income Tax Act rules haven't taken joint custody parents into account. For example, in the case of the married equivalent tax credit, either former spouse, but not both, can claim the credit. For this reason, provisions should be made in the separation agreement for an equitable split of deductions and credits.

Both parents can deduct childcare expenses if they have been separated throughout a taxation year. Each may claim a deduction for the time the child lived with him or her. See Revenue Canada's *Child Care Expenses Tax Guide* for further information.

WHEN SUPPORT PAYMENTS ARE NOT MADE

In shared parenting arrangements, nonpayment of support does not seem to be the problem it has been in sole custody arrangements. Only ten to fifteen percent of the shared parenting respondents in Irving and Benjamin's Shared Parenting Project study reported financial noncompliance as a problematic issue.

If you are not receiving the full amount of support owed to you or are not receiving it at all and have been unable to resolve the problem with your coparent, it may help you to know that some provinces have enacted special legislation and set up programs to assist in the enforcement of support and custody orders. Rather than starting legal enforcement procedures yourself, which cost money and time, you can apply to have your court order enforced by the program office at no cost to you. The office will contact your former spouse and will forward you a government cheque for any monies recovered. If no payment is forthcoming, the department can bring a garnishment order against your former partner's wages. Property or other assets can also be seized and sold. You can withdraw from the program at any time. Look in the Government Blue Pages of your phone book for the office nearest you. If your region does not have this type of program, you might consider placing a clause in your separation agreement to the effect that legal fees for future actions to enforce the agreement will be paid by the former spouse who violates the agreement.

As in all disagreements between parents, children should not be placed in the position of asking the other parent for the support payment. One mother whose former husband was consistently late with payments did tell her child that they couldn't do something because the payment was late. She stated it as a simple fact with no blame attached but no excuses made either.

CHILDREN AND MONEY

When it's my week I give them their allowances and vice versa. The reason for giving the allowances and the amounts of money are different. Their father gives them an allowance for chores and I give them one so that they learn how to handle money.

Marital separation and a lower standard of living unfortunately go hand in hand. In the adjustment period after separation, there may be a temptation to spend money on your child that you can ill afford in an effort to make him feel better. What presents may do, in fact, is pass on the message that material possessions mean love. The best gift you can give your child right now is an emotionally healthy parent who is willing to listen and spend time with him.

Children may worry about your ability to support them. However, if you hide your financial situation from your children, their active imaginations may paint a gloomier picture than actually exists. It's wise to tell your children where the money comes from, where it goes and to ask for their help in cutting down expenses. School-age children can benefit from being shown a simple budget, perhaps with the figures rounded off to make it easier for them to understand. Parents with financial problems may want to let their children know about any steps they are taking to improve the situation.

Dealing emotionally with financial inequalities between the two homes can be difficult for the lower-income parent. In one home, siblings may have to share a room while in the other they have their own rooms. One parent may be able to afford vacation trips while the other cannot. Again, as in all aspects of parenting after divorce, it's important to focus on your child rather than the bitterness and feelings of competitiveness that a difference in standards of living may foster. You may not be able to afford lessons or a computer or sports equipment, but if your coparent is willing to provide them and they benefit your child, maybe that's what you should try to concentrate on rather than your inability to match your former partner's buying power.

Nevertheless, some coparents do take steps to prevent competition. For example, their child's main birthday or Christmas gift may be a joint present. Others make a rule that toys are not given except on special occasions or are paid for by the child out of his allowance. Still others, in allowing their child to take his possessions from one home to the other, prevent the "I have a Superduper Wonder Hero at Dad's. Why can't I have one here?" lament. And finally, sometimes it's helpful to remember that instilling in children a love of nature, reading, music and art is a lifelong gift with no large price tag attached.

Setting Up Two Homes for Your Children

5

I have an "alternative" life-style, and I think my son's feelings of delight and comfort in that life-style would be much less if he didn't also have what everybody else has at his dad's house. He can pick and choose what he likes from each. Although bridging those two worlds can be challenging, it's also very rich.

My parents divorced when I was in my late twenties. Although I was no longer living with them, after the house was sold I had the feeling that I'd lost my "home." It took me a while to realize that "home" is where the people that you love live. And what makes it home are small things — family photos, a favorite armchair, well-loved books, a piece of driftwood collected on a camping trip. When you add objects that your child cherishes or will enjoy, your new home becomes a place where you both belong and can make a new life together.

THE FAMILY HOME

To help children during the adjustment period after separation, some counselors recommend that one parent stay in the family home for awhile if it is financially possible.

The family home's familiar surroundings coupled with familiar household routines provide a sense of security. For parents, there are advantages and disadvantages.

For the parent who stays, there isn't the problem of finding a place to live and moving during a very stressful time. Neighbors who have become friends are close by for support, and the faults of the house or apartment (the leaky faucet, the grumpy landlord) are known factors. On the minus side, the place is full of memories that may make it difficult to begin a new life. If the partner who stays didn't want the separation, the absence of someone in the home is strongly felt.

For the parent who leaves, there is the advantage of making a fresh start in new surroundings. On the other hand, he or she is often blamed by younger children for the separation. In one father's experience, "The kids thought that, because I was the one who left, it had to have been my fault that this awful thing happened to them."

There is also the question of language. Each parent in shared parenting dearly wants his or her child to consider their new accommodation "home." Researcher Isolina Ricci in *Mom's House, Dad's House* recommends using "the other house" or "Mom's or Dad's house" when referring to the other parent's home. This works when both parents have moved. However, when one parent has stayed in the family home, it is difficult for both parents to break the habit of asking, "Do you want to take this home with you?" instead of "Do you want to take this to the other house?" One boy, whose parents have been separated for four years, still considers his father's place, the original family home, "home." Although he calls his mother's house "our house" when they are together, he talks about going "home" to his dad's, not the other way around. It has taken a long time for his mother to accept the fact that no amount of wishful thinking and clever semantics on her part is going to change that. It's a minor irritant. In the end, what is important is that her son is happy in both places and with both parents.

Sometimes one parent is able to retain the family home on a permanent basis. A family member may help with a renegotiated mortgage, or the rent on an apartment may be such that one parent can afford it on his or her salary alone. However, one parent should not be allowed to keep the family home at the expense of the other. In Jeff and Anna's case, their house was extremely important to Jeff. In addition to its significance to him, he felt that, although his children would be living during the week with Anna, on the three weekends out of the four that the boys would be with him the house would provide some stability. After paying Anna her share of the estimated value of the house, he had to remortgage it at a high monthly rate. In their negotiations, the high payments were the justification used for not being able to pay Anna the child support payments she felt she needed. In effect, Jeff's choice to maintain a higher standard of living vis-à-vis accommodation meant a lower standard of living for his former partner and the children.

If you do stay in the family home, try not to change too much all at once. Obviously, you will need to replace some items taken by your coparent, but this isn't the time for a full-scale house makeover. One of the reasons you are staying is to provide some constancy during this time of change. It should go without saying that a child's room is out-of-bounds. Although you may not want to look at your former partner's smiling face beaming from a dresser top, your child does. The same applies to greeting cards sent by your coparent and projects completed together.

When the family home is listed for sale, parents can

help their younger children by being very clear about what is happening to the house and the reasons for the sale. You might begin by telling them that you own the house and are going to sell it, that you will be splitting the money and will use the money to do x, y and z. There are many things that children are uncertain about at this time. The more concrete information you can provide on a level they are capable of understanding, the less they will have to worry about.

MOVING TO A NEW HOME

I was lucky. I moved into a building that seemed to attract single parents right after they had separated. So many of us were in the same situation that it evolved into almost a communal kind of living arrangement. If you had to go to the store, the kids could go across the hall. In some ways the kids preferred living there to living with their father because there were so many kids.

Looking for accommodation after a separation can be an exercise in patience at a time when you have very little. Unless you can afford to buy a more modest house with your share of the family home, you will be looking for a place that you can rent. Unfortunately, in provinces with low vacancy rates (British Columbia, Alberta and Ontario), single parents with children are unlikely to be first on a landlord's list of ideal renters. Here are some strategies that you might consider:

- Be aware of your rights as a potential tenant with children. If there is a tenants' association in your community, call it for information and advice.
- Enlist the help of friends or family to look up ads, make appointments and look at places with you.

- If possible, take a letter of reference from a previous landlord and proof of employment (for example, a stub from a recent pay cheque).
- Be prepared to write a cheque for the first and last month's rent.

Rather than finding an apartment for their family, some single parents decide to share accommodation. Often the cost of renting a house is equivalent or even less than the combined rents of two apartments. Most parents who have done this have found potential housemates among friends, colleagues or acquaintances. The benefits, in addition to saving money, include sharing housekeeping chores, baby-sitting each other's children and providing emotional support to each other. The major drawback is a lack of privacy. Another alternative, if you live in a college town, is renting a room to a student who will help with baby-sitting.

I met a woman who was working in the same office, a university student on a co-op program. She was living with her aunt and really hated it, so I asked her if she would like to come and live at my place. She was a lifesaver. She was the eldest of nine children and she loved kids. Some nights when I came home from work Elise would say, "You're a wreck. Why don't you take a glass of wine and go up and soak in the tub. I'll feed the kids and put them to bed." I would be in the tub listening to her play with the kids. And it makes me want to weep thinking about it because I had absolutely no energy myself to play with them.

Finding accommodation, calling a mover, dividing the household possessions, opening a bank account, arranging for a telephone, sending out change-of-address forms — all the myriad details of moving, plus the emotional trauma of separation, can cause the person who is leaving to overlook what his or her child will need in their new home. If one parent is staying in the family home, it is unlikely that children's items will be divided. And because these items have been built up over the years, they don't readily come to mind. The parent who is moving will need the following, depending upon their child's age:

- First aid kit (thermometer, medicine, bandages, etc.)
- First aid book
- Personal care items (hairbrush, toothbrush, etc.)
- Bedroom furniture, rocking chair, lamp and bedding
- Eating utensils for a preschooler
- Clothing if you are going to have a set in each home; if not, a pair of pajamas, underwear, socks and at least one set of clothes to cut down on the amount of clothing that moves back and forth and for emergencies
- Basic school supplies (pencils, pens, paper, etc.)
- Vaporizer
- Car seat
- Potty seat or adapter if child is being toilet-trained
- Diapering and feeding equipment and supplies for babies and toddlers

Once a second home has been set up, it is important for the child to see it as soon as possible so that he knows where his other parent is living and where he will be living. Be forewarned, though. Your child's introduction to his new home is bound to be awkward. My own son's was little short of disastrous. We opened the door of the house to find the kitchen ceiling in danger of collapsing from a leaky pipe in the bathroom. I spent the first half hour mopping up water, all the time trying to convince myself that it just had to get better from that point on. Assuming that you won't be met with a flood, you can ease the awkwardness of the visit by getting your child involved in setting up this new home for both of you. By asking his advice and giving him options about where his bed should be placed, where a picture should be hung in his room or where his belongings should go, he will feel that he has some say in his new life. Only by feeling needed and a part of your new beginning will he grow to feel a sense of belonging in two homes.

Feeling comfortable in the neighborhood is also important for a youngster, especially if your new home is in an area with which he's unfamiliar. As soon as you can, you should make a tour of the area with your child, introducing him to neighbors and potential playmates you have met, the local Block Parents and the corner variety store merchant. This is also the time to set boundaries and establish areas that are off-limits.

Before your family actually starts shared parenting, you will need to decide what travels from one home to the other. This often depends on the time-sharing plan you have negotiated. Parents who choose a "one week with Mom, one week with Dad" plan generally have a set of clothes in each home. Coats, special occasion outfits and boots make the trip back and forth although on the first day it snows the boots will inevitably be at the other parent's. With a more frequent plan, some or all items of clothing are often sent with the child. This involves some stocktaking once in a while to discover the whereabouts of errant socks and sweatshirts, not to mention gritting one's teeth about the laundry abilities of former mates. Parents who don't see their children as frequently have found that keeping an emergency set of clothing at their home is a good idea.

We each have the children for a week at a time and pick them up at school on the changeover day. When we first separated, I left most of their clothes with their father and bought new ones. I liked the feeling of starting fresh. Generally, we don't ask the kids to cart things back and forth. I drop things off or their father does—boots, snowsuits, that kind of thing. They have toys at both houses. Our daughter has two stuffed animals that go back and forth. She puts those in the backpack she takes to school.

A child's possessions belong to him, not the household. Although you may have spent a minor fortune on a toy for your child, if he wants to keep it at his other home for whatever reason, he should be allowed to do so. And if he wants to cart toys back and forth, that should also be up to him. Depending upon his age, a child can learn to be responsible for his own belongings. You can help him remember what to take with him on the changeover day by asking him to make a list the evening before. A large calendar at each home, with lessons, games, dates library books are due and other activities and important dates marked on it, will help your child in drawing up his checklist. One of the best calendars I've seen for children is a reusable laminated wall calendar called the Edu-Calendar. It is available for $19.50 (including shipping and handling) in a teddy bear or dinosaur motif and comes with a water-soluble marker and forty cling-vinyl stickers illustrating birthday parties and other events. To order contact: Tasara, 2341 Queen Street East, Suite 105, Toronto, Ontario M4E 1H2.

STRESS DURING THE ADJUSTMENT PERIOD

We had two dogs and a cat. I took the cat, and I was terrified it would run away from my new apartment. It was so important to me that the cat be there because it seemed such a symbol of stability. It stayed for a month and then ran away just when the kids were about to go to their father's. I spent the whole week just devastated because I kept thinking how awful this was going to be for the kids. They never even missed the cat. It was a day or so before they even realized the cat was gone and their reaction was just ho-hum. I used up all that energy worrying about a stupid cat!

There is no easy cure-all for dealing with the stress of beginning a new life, but there may be some lessons to be learned from those who have been through the divorce process before you. Most divorced parents will tell you that it takes time to see yourself as a single person rather than a married one and to feel secure with that new self-image. It also takes time for you and your children to rebuild the image that you have of your family. In the past, society has said that children whose parents have divorced came from "broken homes." Rejecting this view is one way to throw off the label of "failure" that some uninformed people will try to attach to you. Divorce doesn't mean the failure of a marriage or the end of a family; it simply means the end of a marriage and a family's reorganization into a different type of family, what one researcher calls a "binuclear family." Rather than finding new labels, however, some family counselors are suggesting that maybe it's time we started to view a family as a group of people who love and care for one another rather than the traditional view of a group of people related by blood or marriage.

Thinking positively about your new status and your family's is a goal reached by taking small steps each day. As a family begins shared parenting, even minor problems may seem insurmountable. Many parents admit to feeling that they coped inadequately during this time. "You do the best you can," is a frequent comment. Researcher Judith Wallerstein has found that "during the early stages of separation and divorce, children find that their mothers and fathers are much less available as parents; the adults' attention is focused elsewhere." To break away from this pattern involves beginning to find pleasure in your own small accomplishments — mastering a new task, going to a movie on your own — and continuing a relationship with your child in a new setting or under new circumstances.

Some parents caution against expecting or attempting too much, too soon. People leave their marriages to make better lives for themselves and their children. When everything doesn't run as smoothly as they had hoped it would, they can become discouraged. One mother remembers being obsessed about making her new home as comfortable as possible for her children. The first week they were with her was fine, but she was heartbroken when, on their return after a week with their father, her preschooler couldn't remember where the bathroom was or where the toys were kept. She desperately wanted their lives to "return to normal." Another parent, ignoring the emotional drain of a separation, decided to switch jobs, adding more stress to an already stressful situation — "In retrospect, it wasn't a good time to make a move. I think my job suffered because of my mental state, the terrible drain that separation can be. I think people lose themselves after a separation and it takes a considerable amount of time to get back to where you were."

During this adjustment period, it is important to discuss with your coparent how your child has been reacting to the separation when he is with you and how you responded. If the other parent was the one who wanted to end the marriage, it may be difficult to describe the child's reaction or behavior in a nonaccusatory way. But playing the game of "Let's see how guilty we can make the other person feel" turns the discussion into an argument about your marriage rather than one whose focus should be finding solutions to your child's problems.

One of the best ways to help your child is by showing him that you are still capable of taking care of him. In the first few days after her separation, one mother recalls being so depressed that she was unable to feed her children. Her six-year-old son fed his four-year-old sister peanut butter sandwiches until the peanut butter and bread ran out. It isn't unusual for parents to feel paralyzed by fear or depression at this stage. Caring for their children, working, making meals and doing household chores seem to take an enormous amount of energy. However, faced with a parent who doesn't seem able to function, children are understandably afraid. During this crisis phase, their basic needs are simple food, clean clothes, a bed to sleep in and the knowledge that their parents love them. They need to be told that the sadness a parent feels was not caused by them and that a parent is attempting to solve the problems he or she has. They need to see that their parents are still responsible adults who can take care of themselves and their children.

Although each family will find its own way of coping with stress during this period, you might consider some of the following:

- Exercise is a great stress-reliever. If financially possible, try to ensure that you all continue the activities that you took part in before the separation. Or find something active to do together (skating, swimming, playing catch, bicycling). During this time, one mother and her five-year-old son began going for a walk on

Sunday evenings when they were together. He chose the route and both enjoyed it so much that, two years later, it is still part of their routine. Community centers often have family activities — family gym or swims — for a nominal fee.

- At first, try to tackle one major household chore a week. No one has ever died from living in a messy house. Likewise, no one has ever died from not eating three cooked meals a day. Simple meals can be just as nutritious as complicated ones.

- Family therapists suggest that, when parents arrive home from work, they spend the first fifteen minutes or so with their children, reading a story, playing or talking, rather than immediately starting dinner. It gives everyone a chance to unwind. You might also consider setting aside a special time during the week to be with each of your children. When a child is under stress, even a short time experiencing a parent's undivided attention can be beneficial.

- Consider using relaxation techniques, such as controlled breathing, tightening and relaxing various muscle groups or visualization. There are numerous books and courses available on these techniques. For courses available in your community, check the "Stress Management and Counseling" section of the Yellow Pages or contact your local community college.

- Parents and children under stress are more vulnerable to infections. Although sleep and diet patterns are bound to be disrupted at this time, it is a good idea to try to follow a healthy diet and ensure that each member of the family gets enough sleep.

- The support of friends is important for children and parents. It's tempting but destructive to retreat into a shell at this time. Children can be reminded that their friends are welcome in both homes. Parents shouldn't be shy about contacting friends. One mother cautions against burdening just one friend with all of your problems, though — "Spread it around!" Continuing to attend groups that you went to as an individual during the marriage can also be helpful. After his separation, one father continued to meet with a group of male friends once a week and found their support invaluable at a time when he was finding shared parenting a big challenge.

- All parents who share custody of their children recommend cultivating a sense of humor to get you through the rough patches.

If, during this time, you find that your friends are unable to be objective about your situation, or you need a fresh perspective, or you or your children are in distress, individual counseling or group therapy may help you and your child feel less alone.

SEEKING HELP FOR YOUR CHILD OR YOURSELF

Jenny seemed to do quite well at first, but just before she turned four, she had a terrible outburst and managed to verbalize her feelings of responsibility for the situation. We all had a few sessions with a counselor, who concluded that Jenny was doing just fine, but her parents probably had some things to work out! Jenny felt relieved. Here was a person outside the family who managed to give her confidence that she wasn't the only child who lived in two homes and that it wasn't her fault.

Seeking help for your child or yourself is a sign of strength and responsibility rather than a sign of weakness or failure as a parent. Long gone are the days when going to counseling implied that you were suffering from mental illness.

Depending upon the size of your community, help is available through individual counseling or discussion groups. In larger communities there may be counseling services specifically for divorced families. To find out if one is available in your community, contact your local family service association. Your local social service agency is a good place to start in any case. Their counselors will be familiar with the resources in the community and can help you with external stresses, such as finding day care and housing, as well as the internal stresses caused by a marriage ending. A counselor will listen to your problems and help you find ways to deal with them.

Counseling is also available through private practice counselors — psychiatrists, psychologists, social workers and other therapists. Psychiatrists have a medical degree and training in psychiatry and are the only counselors who can dispense drugs. Psychologists have a PhD and practice psychotherapy. Social workers usually have a degree at the master's level (MSW) and training in individual and family dynamics. A minister or rabbi with good counseling skills can also be helpful at this time.

Because anyone can claim to be an individual or family counselor, it is wise to adopt a consumer approach to finding a therapist. Even if someone has been recommended to you, it is a good idea to ask the following questions on the telephone or during an initial consultation. You may not feel comfortable asking all of them, but remember that you are paying for the service either directly or through your taxes. (You might consider checking your health coverage at work to see if counseling is included in the plan.)

- How long have you been a therapist or counselor?
- What is your training?
- Have you had any experience working with people undergoing divorce?
- What hours do you work?
- What are your fees? Is there a charge for the initial consultation? How much notice must be given if an appointment has to be cancelled, and what is charged for missed appointments?
- What approaches or techniques do you use in your work?

You may also ask personal questions such as the therapist's age, marital status and whether he or she has children, although therapists sometimes choose not to answer such questions.

Once you know that a counselor is qualified, the next step is arranging an initial consultation. At that time you should decide whether or not you feel comfortable talking to this counselor. Do you feel that you can be open and honest with him or her about your feelings and problems? At the end of the interview, the counselor should be able to give you an idea of a plan and a time frame. You should have a clear understanding of how the counselor arrived at the plan and why he or she thinks that plan is the best one for you.

Some parents find group discussions with other divorced parents helpful during this transition phase. Finding out that other parents share your concerns, feelings and problems can be a wonderful morale booster. Again, contact your local social service agency for information on seminars for newly divorced parents in your area.

Seeking help for a child involves a similar process.

Individual counselors and group leaders should be questioned about their qualifications and experience, particularly whether or not they have experience with children whose parents are separated or divorced. If you decide upon group rather than individual therapy, the group's aims, size and the age of its members should be verified. You should also find out what their practice concerning confidentiality is and whether or not there is follow-up service available. Knowing that they aren't the only ones whose parents are separated and talking with other children in the same situation is often helpful for school-age children and adolescents. However, you should find out from the group leader if this type of therapy would be suitable for your child. Meeting with other children in a group situation sounds appealing but, depending upon your child's problem, may in fact not be appropriate. Group discussions for children range from single, two-hour workshops such as the one held by the Family Conciliation services of Manitoba Community Services, to six-session therapy groups for children with concurrent groups for parents offered by the Families in Transition department of the Family Service Association of Metropolitan Toronto. In general, groups discuss how families change when parents separate, support children to build self-confidence, and provide an opportunity to teach new ways of coping with the difficult situations presented by changing family circumstances.

How do you decide if your child needs counseling? Pediatrician T. Berry Brazelton offers guidelines in his book *Families: Crisis and Caring.* "Therapy for an individual child should be considered when the child is frightened or withdraws and cannot be reached by the parents, or when emotional or psychosomatic symptoms interfere with his or her functioning—in school, with peers, or with siblings. If a child seems not to play actively, or to be enjoying it less, this can also be a warning sign. . . . Another sign that a child needs help is the reactions of other children. If they consistently shy away, they are sensing the child's upset. He or she will, in turn, sense their rejection, and this can become a vicious cycle of isolation."

In many situations, we give our children choices, but this is one time when professionals agree that it is better not to. In a quiet moment, a parent might simply say, "Your father [or mother] and I have decided we need to consult someone about our life. We're going to see someone who knows a lot about children and can help us solve some of our problems." School-age children and teenagers may resist quite strenuously. If they do, parents can assure them that their feelings are understood but that they are expected to go and give it a chance.

DEVELOPING A PARENTING PARTNERSHIP

Ritzy was found underneath our porch by Christopher a month before we separated. We tried to make him into a joint custody cat and it almost cost us the joint custody of our son. About a year into the arrangement, my ex decided that joint custody wasn't going to work for us. We went to a mediator, and within a meeting we figured out that it all had to do with this cat going back and forth. I ended up with sole custody of the cat and now everything is fine.

Setting up a parenting partnership and finding ways to settle your differences are two essential ingredients for making shared parenting work.

Many family experts recommend developing a businesslike relationship with your coparent. Many parents, on the other hand, balk at the idea, especially in the early stages of a separation. It seems too calculated, too unnatural. Those who parted on fairly good terms wonder why they shouldn't still talk about their private lives with their former partners. Those who parted as enemies don't see why they should be expected to conduct a polite conversation with someone who hurt them deeply. Neither has begun what Isolina Ricci in *Mom's House, Dad's House* calls "the retreat from intimacy." To be emotionally free from the other parent is the first step in building a working relationship as parents. Treating your former spouse as a parenting partner helps this separation process.

At first, counselors suggest that a parent try to imagine his or her coparent as a coworker. In the workplace we often have to cooperate with someone we are uncomfortable with for reasons ranging from incompatibility to active dislike. Our relationship with that person is usually businesslike and polite with the odd angry flare-up to be smoothed over on both sides. Here are some suggestions to keep in mind when embarking on this new relationship with your former mate:

- Times should be arranged to discuss important matters. Phoning a coparent at work or at home without warning is unfair. If transition times involve seeing the other parent, this is also a bad time to start a discussion. It's better to phone the other person to set up a time to talk in the evening after the children are in bed.
- A parent who feels himself slipping into unbusinesslike behavior during a conversation should say so and agree to talk again at a later time. Phoning when you are affected by alcohol or other drugs, or at stressful times of the day, should also be avoided. And when the actions

of one parent have angered the other, it's a good idea to wait until the anger has subsided and then phone to set up a time to discuss the problem.

- Children should never be used as messengers in an attempt to avoid direct communication with a coparent. It is unfair to them. They may get the message confused or they may forget to deliver it. If a parent has an important message or simply a reminder, it helps the entire family to write it down to give to the other parent. Parents who find that they are at a disadvantage in a conversation with their coparent often find letters a good way to communicate their feelings about important issues. Prearranged calls, notes and letters are mature, businesslike ways to communicate.

- We don't expect or need approval of our actions from coworkers who are not friends; however, a compliment on a job well done is usually appreciated and helps build goodwill. In the same way, when your coparent has done something to bolster your child's self-esteem or has made an extra effort for whatever reason, try to acknowledge it.

- Coparents should attempt to keep appointments or promises. Not doing so can sometimes lead to retaliation, which is emotionally unhealthy for all concerned. This can be verbal retaliation along the lines of "I'm not surprised your father didn't do what he said he would. He's not to be trusted." It also includes not being flexible about switching weekends when an important event comes up for the coparent.

- Respecting a coparent's privacy is important. You would not expect to hear the details of a coworker's private life any more than you would want to divulge details of yours. Nor should you pump your children for details. Later on in your relationship with your coparent you may feel more comfortable discussing matters other than your children, but such discussions should be mutually agreed upon.

Even when these guidelines are followed, it's unlikely that your partnership will experience completely smooth sailing. Some problems you will just have to learn to accept and others will require action on your part.

We all know that you can't change someone else's basic personality, yet some of us still try, even after divorce. If one parent was unconcerned about cracker crumbs on the rug and spider webs on the ceiling before the divorce, he or she is unlikely to be any different now that the couple live apart. The same holds true for absent-minded bill-payers, rigid schedule-setters and junk food addicts. Worrying about the effect on your children of what you consider to be the bad character traits of their other parent and ordering him or her to shape up are counterproductive to say the least. All this will do is to raise the stress level of all concerned. It's far better to relax and acknowledge that the behavior probably bothers you more than it does your children.

When parents begin shared parenting, it is often difficult for them to accept the fact that the other parent has legal control over their children while they are with him or her. If plans have been made to take your six-year-old to a movie that you believe is unsuitable for her age group, you can voice your disapproval but little more. How you express your reservations is important to the ongoing relationship you are building. Setting up an appointment to talk, asking questions to ensure you have your facts straight, stating your opinion calmly and fairly and listening to the other parent's viewpoint will help you to avoid having the conversation turn into a power struggle. In the case of a movie, your coparent may simply be unaware of its unsuitability. Harsh criticism that puts your coparent on the defensive may backfire, doing more to ensure that the child will go to the movie than preventing it from happening.

What does a parent do, though, if a coparent is not following through with what he or she agreed to in their separation agreement? If support payments aren't being made, there are several steps a parent can take (see page 77). If the problem has to do with an issue such as the coparent consistently not taking the child when he or she has agreed to, and you have met several times and there has still been no improvement, a family counselor or mediator (see page 50) may be able to help.

There are other circumstances in which legal measures can and must be taken. For example, it is terrifying for children to have to deal with parents who are out of control due to drug or alcohol abuse. It is clearly unsafe as well. Depending upon the situation, you have a legal responsibility to contact the police, the Children's Aid Society or a lawyer if you believe that your children are in danger.

GUIDELINES FOR COPARENTS

There are certain guidelines that parents involved in shared parenting can follow to make their children's and their own lives as trouble-free as possible.

■ *Avoid criticizing the other parent.*
When you get into joint custody you have to say to yourself that you'll never criticize the other parent in front of the child. Somehow you have to find positive things to say to make sure your child continues to respect his other parent, that he

doesn't become disillusioned just because you did. But when you do that and start saying those things, you start believing them yourself a little bit. It has an interesting feedback effect.

Although we had a few arguments in front of the children, it wasn't too bad. I didn't put their father down. Even now I wouldn't put him down. I believe that anything you drop in a child's mind and keep repeating stays there and becomes reality for them.

A child's sense of identity is closely tied to his sense of who his parents are. Both parents are thus role models for their child. This is why family counselors recommend that parents not criticize each other in front of their children and why many longtime coparents will point to this as a basic ground rule in their shared parenting arrangement.

For a child, what you don't say can be as significant as what you do say. There may be some small satisfaction gained in hanging up the phone without saying good-bye or not saying hello when the other parent comes to your home, but what does this convey to your child? Simply that this person doesn't deserve the courtesy that a stranger is given. Although a parent may, for whatever reason, not feel like being polite to his or her former partner, courteous behavior is called for for their child's sake.

Criticism may take indirect forms as well, undermining the confidence of a child in his or her parent. For example, six-year-old Sara had fallen off some playground equipment while with her mother. When she arrived at her father's house, the first thing that he noticed was the bump on her forehead. After asking her what had happened, the father pointedly asked, "Was your mother watching you?" This type of remark is unnecessary unless a parent truly believes that the other parent isn't providing adequate care. Even then, the problem should be discussed in private with the other parent.

Direct criticism of one parent by the other is probably the most harmful to a child. In *Helping Your Child Succeed After Divorce*, family counselor Florence Bienenfeld writes that "because most children are attached to both parents, each unkind remark is like a blow felt by them. Aside from frightening them and making them miserable, imagine what this teaches them about life and about relationships. The images of this conflict will remain with them forever." Children who are recovering from the pain of their parents' separation cannot heal in this type of atmosphere.

This isn't to say that a parent shouldn't be honest with a child about his or her feelings about the other parent; however, there is a difference between being honest and attacking the other parent as a person. Your children already know their parents are no longer happy together. Saying that you are angry with their father because he's late is not the same as calling him an irresponsible lout who was never on time a day in his life. Saying to him when he arrives that you need to talk about the problem with him later is better than confronting him with angry words in front of your children. Before you prepare to do battle, it's worthwhile to remember that how your children eventually treat the opposite sex will be drawn, in part, from what they witness in their parents' relationship.

Some children actively try to prevent parental conflict. They avoid issues they think will cause problems between their parents. Older children may discourage criticism of one parent by the other. Or they may take the opposite tack and tell each parent what they think he or she wants to hear. Children shouldn't have to protect themselves from their parents' anger toward each other. Although divorce is a difficult time and controlling every disparaging remark is unrealistic, coparents should make a special effort.

■ *Avoid placing a child in the middle of an argument.*

In some cases the child is the focus of an argument and becomes trapped in the middle or is forced to choose sides. Because most children of divorce are intensely loyal toward both parents, this places them in an emotionally harmful position.

One father had taken his preschooler to the beach. Just as he brought her to her mother's home, his daughter wet her pants. As the mother hustled her into the bathroom, she noticed that her daughter's running shoes were wet and told her that she would have to put on her sandals. As the little girl began to cry over the removal of her favorite shoes, the father, forgetting for the moment that the child had had an accident, said that he didn't see how her shoes could have gotten wet because she hadn't gone near the water. The mother saw this as an attempt to undermine her authority and an argument began over a very minor problem. The daughter at first happily sided with her father, but then as the two adults became involved in their quarrel, she wandered away, confused and ignored. If the parents had discussed the problem later, instead of in front of their daughter, she would not have been caught in the middle.

■ *Time-share in a reasonable way that meets children's needs.*

I tend to be more flexible. If Nora is invited to a birthday party by her cousin on her dad's side, and it's my weekend, I would tend to say, "Sure, go ahead." Her dad isn't flexible that way. Recently I've tried once or twice, but I have to accept that he is reluctant to make changes. If it's something major — a vacation week having to be rescheduled around work — that's one thing, but generally I sense he'd rather I not ask.

In an ideal world, both coparents would be flexible people, and in fact, some parents are very relaxed about changing the schedule to suit the needs of the other parent or their children. However, in some shared parenting relationships, one person is rule- and schedule-oriented and the other isn't. As the mother quoted above found, it is easier to accept the rigidity of the other parent than attempt to change it.

Generally, it is the small changes in schedule that occur with little forewarning that cause problems. If a parent must change the schedule for a legitimate reason, he or she should talk to the other parent and child as soon as possible. We have all heard stories of children waiting to be picked up by a parent, only to have the parent not come. There is a loss of trust experienced by the child as well as great disappointment and a feeling of insecurity. When the schedule is changed, it is not unusual for a child to insist on a day missed with one parent being made up for at some other time. This appeals to the sense of fairness that develops in the middle childhood years.

■ **Make transitions as easy as possible.**
Seeing my former husband every day was very difficult. I think where possible, it's to be avoided. In the beginning, you're still so angry with each other that to have daily contact is just setting yourself up to be hurt or upset.

Transitions from one home to the other can be one of the most difficult aspects of parenting after divorce. However, coparents have found that there are a number of steps that can be taken to reduce the stress when children first arrive and when they are preparing to leave for their other home.

First, you can help prepare your child for the time away from you by being positive about his or her stay with the other parent. In the beginning, there is a tendency to overemphasize how much you will miss your child. The child starts to worry about how you will survive without him and how lonely you'll be, with the result that your parting can be emotionally draining for both of you. If your relationship with your coparent is barely cordial, it may also be difficult to let your child know that you want him to have a good time at his other home. As much as you are ashamed to admit it, there may even be a tiny part of you that hopes your child has a lousy time. Many parents must deal with that slippery slope of competition for their child's affection. Part of it is tied in with angry feelings toward the former spouse and part of it is the hope that the child would prefer to stay with the parent he is leaving. In both cases, you are concentrating on negative feelings about the former partner rather than on the needs of the child.

Second, you can ease a child's return by being courteous with the other parent and leaving any complaints about lateness or whatever for another time. For example, in one family, the father is somewhat casual about his five-year-old daughter's appearance. He is awkward with barrettes and rarely notices if an outfit is worn with its matching belt. Inevitably, these lapses are commented upon by his coparent as soon as he and his daughter enter the other home. It has evolved into a pattern that makes transitions from one home to the other stressful.

Third, seasoned coparents have learned that it is

important not to overwhelm a child with hugs, questions and chatter as soon as the youngster enters the home. It takes children a while to adjust to being in their other home and this should be respected. They like to wander around at first to see if anything has changed. God forbid if someone has tripped over a building block castle and broken it in their absence! What to you may be transitory playthings to them are signs of permanence and belonging — their things in their home — and they like to ensure that they are still all there.

For parents who don't want to see each other on changeover days, the following are possible solutions. Older children can go to their other home by themselves. One parent can deliver a child to school or day care on a weekday morning (often Monday or Friday) to be picked up by the other parent in the afternoon. A young child who is being cared for by his mother during the day can be taken to a neighbor's to be picked up there by his father.

■ *Respect each other's privacy.*

One day I hurried straight from the factory to pick up my son on time. After I arrived at his mother's apartment, I went down the hall to use the bathroom. The following week Domenic told me that his mother didn't like me using the bathroom there. At first, I thought this was unreasonable and petty, but then I realized that it really was an invasion of her privacy.

There is a difference between casually waltzing into the other parent's home and being invited by the child and coparent. In fact, it is often beneficial for a child to be able to share this part of his life with the other parent. Although neither David nor I is especially comfortable in the other's home, I have marveled over a hot rod and the new fish at David's, and he has oohed and aahed over a block building and the new turtles at my house, and Mark has played the proud host on all occasions. Sometimes it is worth a bit of awkwardness to see the pride in your child's face. However, this is partly a function of time and the relationship you have with your coparent.

I don't think it's crucial for me to see my daughter's bedroom in her other home. But it was very important for her to draw the layout of her father's house to show me. She also shows me photographs she's taken there. I don't believe it's important for me to go into her father's house or for him to enter mine. I don't want to put Peter or myself in a difficult position, and I think that is something we can ask of our children.

■ **Cooperate with respect to activities.**

I'm anxious for my son to get into hockey and learn something about it, and his mother is just as anxious not to have anything to do with it. Cameron isn't interested. He'd be good at it if he tried and I want him to try, but without his mother's cooperation, there's not much I can do. It really boils down to the fact that I can't act independently. The hockey leagues don't want you if you're not there every week. What we have all agreed on is a power-skating course. I hope I will eventually be able to work him into some kind of hockey.

Children's activities are very important to them and, like their toys or other belongings, belong to them and not their parents. It doesn't matter which parent organized the activity; both should cooperate to ensure that their child is able to continue playing sports, taking lessons or attending group meetings.

If a new activity is considered and rejected by the other parent and child as in the quotation above, compromises must be reached or the issue dropped. In the case that a parent and child are interested in a new activity but the other parent isn't, the interested parent could assume the responsibility of taking the child to the activity regardless of the time-sharing schedule.

At times a child will be caught between the opposing wishes of his parents. One mother specified in their separation agreement that her son attend a camp that she had attended as a child. The following summer, in addition to being sent to his mother's old camp, the boy was sent by his father to a different camp. The second summer after the separation, the son had to choose one camp over the other. Communication between parents avoids placing children in this type of awkward position.

Discussion in advance also prevents problems regarding who will attend dinners, championship games and ceremonies of various types. Most children want both parents at these types of functions and most coparents comply. Those who have a barely cordial relationship generally put on their polite social masks and pat themselves on the back afterward for being so decent. After all, it's hardly fair to turn a child's happy occasion into an embarrassing moment for her when her parents won't speak to each other in front of her friends. If you think this will be the case, decide on which parent will attend, or attend at different times.

■ *Let your child talk freely.*

For a long time Matthew didn't talk about his life with his mom. It's not that he isn't supposed to talk about it, but I think he sensed that I was uncomfortable hearing about things and possibly vice versa. Now we're both much more open, and he's able to tell stories about interesting things that happened in his other home.

There certainly aren't any restrictions against his talking about his life during the week away from us, but most eleven-year-old boys are pretty tight-lipped anyway. He likes to tease us about his father's car and how much better it is than ours.

After a separation, some parents move bravely ahead with their new lives, while others take much longer to begin again. The first group puts the past firmly away while the second group reluctantly returns to it again and again. Neither group wants to listen to their children talk about "the time we did this" or "the time we visited so-and-so." But it is necessary to listen. The past is important to children and they should be allowed to share good memories of when their family lived together, no matter how painful those memories are for parents.

It's also important that a child feel comfortable talking about the time he spends with his other parent. If he is told that you'd rather not hear about what he does at his other home, your relationship won't be full and open because you have placed boundaries on it. Although you may want your life to be as separate as possible from your coparent's, your child's life flows from one home to the other. Events at one home may have an effect on events at the other. Or your child may want to share something learned at the other home. It may be difficult, particularly early in a separation or when your coparent has formed a new relationship, to listen to stories about your child's other life, but a child should feel free to share triumphs, sorrows, new adventures and concerns with each parent.

Placing restrictions on what a child can tell his other parent about his life with you is the other side of the coin. Emphasizing the importance of not telling a coparent something almost ensures that it will be passed along.

A corollary to allowing a child to talk freely about his other life is allowing him to bring items from the other home to yours; for example, items that he and his other parent have made together. I'm not talking about a six-foot cardboard playhouse — lines have to be drawn somewhere! — but items that hold significance for your child and that he wants to share with you or just have with him at his other home. One of the saddest stories I've heard was of a four-year-old girl who was given an old scarf of her father's to wear on their drive to her mother's house. The child took great pleasure in wearing the scarf and her father told her that she could keep it. When they arrived, the little girl rushed to her mother in another room to show off her new possession, but then returned to the hallway in tears. Her mother had told her it was an adult scarf and should be returned to her father.

■ Respect each other's religious views.

If one parent believes in organized religion and the other doesn't, it is important to respect the other's view and his or her right to share it with your child. Generally, children in such families attend services every other weekend if this is the time-sharing arrangement. Again, attending religious services should be considered another one of the child's activities. If an important service is being held on a weekend when the child is with his other parent and he wants to go, permission should be given.

■ Respect each other's rules.

We tend to allow the smutty ten-year-old humor here; in fact, I often provide the second verse if he doesn't know it! That's not tolerated at his other home. On the other hand, we stress table manners and they don't. We always notice the difference in him on the changeover day. It's always "Don't talk with your mouth full," and "Elbows off the table." By the end of the week, he's fine and then the whole cycle starts again.

Children will accept different rules in their two homes if the rules are upheld consistently and if the parents don't criticize each other's standards. However, some parents have found that if a child is complaining — not just for the sake of complaining but for valid reasons — it's a good idea to listen and consider changing a rule to conform to the other household.

HOLIDAYS AND SPECIAL OCCASIONS

The sensible thing to do about holidays, children's birthdays and other important events is to sit down at the beginning of each year with your coparent and a calendar and work out a schedule for the entire year. If your child is in school, it's often a good idea to plan from September to September so that you can take into account teachers' Professional Activity days as well as school holidays. Although some people plan ahead for each holiday or special occasion, most are casual about the minor holidays, letting them fall where they may, and alternate or share the ones that are important to them. If there are two or more days of celebration during a religious festival, some parents split the holiday. For instance, Jewish children might spend the first day of Rosh Hashanah with their mother and the second day with their father.

Being flexible can make everyone's life easier. Halloween is a good example. Sometimes a child has friends close by at her other home and wants to go out trick-or-treating with them. A coparent in this situation might help the child with her costume, take a photo, let her visit a few of the neighbors she likes on the street and then take her to the coparent's. If this calls for more organization than the two parents can muster, the other parent can simply pick the child up after school.

At winter holiday time, the calendars of shared parenting families are a mass of indecipherable "who goes where when" scribbles. Nerves are frazzled, emotions are running high and you may wish you were on some South Seas island—anywhere but home for the holidays.

Sharing the holiday can have unforeseen difficulties. Jim and Barbara had separated when Stephanie was three. For the next three years, Stephanie spent Christmas Eve and morning with her dad and Christmas afternoon, dinner and overnight with her mom. At the age of six, when both parents had formed new relationships, there was some talk of alternating the entire holiday, but Stephanie was adamant. She liked spending part of Christmas with each parent and wanted that to continue. Taking their daughter's wishes into account, the parents agreed that they would keep the split holiday schedule but alternate it every year.

Alternating Christmas can have its own problems. When they separated, Dan and Cheryl had decided to alternate Christmases, with the nonparticipating parent opening gifts with the child a few days afterward. They had also agreed that Santa would visit both houses. Unfortunately, what each gave the child was not discussed in advance. By the time Dan had talked to Cheryl, she and her relatives had bought every item on Tara's "wish" list. Since the first Christmas following the separation fell on

Dan's weekend, Tara ran downstairs to discover that Santa hadn't left anything that she had written on her list. Although it was explained that perhaps Santa had left those toys at her mother's house, there was an air of disappointment and confusion surrounding what should have been a happy event.

Experienced coparents and family counselors suggest the following ways to alleviate stress during holidays:

- Try to get away from the "my holiday, your holiday" mentality and think of it as your child's holiday. If your coparent wants to call his child to wish her a Merry Christmas or Happy Hanukkah or Happy Easter, consider setting up a time that won't disrupt your festivities. Older children and adolescents can be given a say in holiday planning with final decisions remaining with the parents.

- Accept that you are not going to be able to accommodate every relative if the holiday is shared. Rushing from one relative's home to the next makes everyone ill-tempered.

- Discuss gifts ahead of time. For example, large presents, such as a bicycle for a school-age child or an expensive piece of clothing for a teenager, could be joint purchases to keep costs down and to avoid double purchases.

- If you are not spending the holiday with your child, help her to feel comfortable about the arrangement and not worry about you. Get together with friends or relatives and let your child know that you will not be alone. Knowing that you will be OK on the holiday allows her to enjoy it too.

- Beginning new traditions can often be less stressful than continuing old ones. For ideas, ask your librarian or your local bookseller for books on holiday crafts and activities. At Easter you might consider making an Easter tree to celebrate new beginnings. Pussy willows or forsythia branches or just plain sticks are placed in a jar or vase, decorated with tissue paper cherry blossoms and then hung with decorated eggs. In our family, we're too lazy to do the eggs properly, so we save eggshells, paint them with watercolors and hang them.

Summer vacations must be planned well in advance so that childcare can be arranged during the times when both parents are working. If Christmases are alternated, a weekend is usually switched and the schedule readjusted in the summer.

One last point. In the beginning, it may be difficult to get into the habit again of taking pictures of your child on special occasions. There can be a terrible sense of loss and loneliness on holidays, but taking photographs, even just a few, indicates to your child that this holiday is as important as all the others that went before and that your times with her are precious and worth preserving.

BIRTHDAYS

Coparents handle birthdays in various ways. Some alternate birthdays, with the nonparticipating parent and child celebrating on another day. Having two birthday parties is seldom a cause for despair for children; in fact, they often brag to friends about it, particularly if the two celebrations result in additional gifts. Other coparents share the day.

Sharing the day can take many forms. One former couple, whose little girl loves sleepover parties, divide the party into two parts. The mother, who is a better cook than the father, holds the traditional party at her home.

The father is part of the festivities there and then takes his daughter and her friends to his home, which is larger and more suitable for the sleepover part of the celebration.

For parents who feel uncomfortable in each other's homes but who still want to share the day with their child, there are a number of venues to choose from, from popular restaurants to picnics in the park. Some YMCAs have a birthday party program for younger children. They provide treat bags, balloons, drinks and staff to supervise for about $12 a child. There are also indoor playgrounds in some communities. These mostly cater to younger children and tend to be expensive. They usually have a ball bath, climbing equipment, riding cars, an electric train, slides, a playhouse, a play kitchen, blocks, puzzles and toys.

For Mark's sixth birthday, David and I rented a local pool for an hour and held the rest of the birthday party at his house. I sent out the invitations and provided the food and David decorated the house and bought the treat bags. This isn't something that we would have felt comfortable with the first year of our separation, but now it feels fine.

LONG-DISTANCE PARENTING

Even when I was away for just a few days, I'd send each of my children a postcard. Or T-shirts with the name of the place I was visiting. When I wrote them a letter, I'd send them a postcard in the envelope. They're grown up now, but both saved all those postcards, so they must have been important to them.

There are times when a parent must be away from his or her child for longer than the normal span of time between stays. A child should be given as much advance warning as possible if this is the case. The parent who is away can keep in touch by sending tapes, letters and postcards and phoning at regular, prearranged times. The parent who is with the child can encourage him to write letters and send artwork and tapes. The child should also be permitted to phone the other parent. (It can be worked out in advance who will pay for the calls.)

When a parent must be out of town for a long time, a child may need to travel alone to visit him or her. The airlines generally allow a child to travel unaccompanied after the age of five; however, you should check with your airline regarding their rules for children traveling alone and the minimum age required for stopover flights. Be sure to provide your child with a good variety of things to do on the flight—a backpack can be used to hold activity books, books for reading, markers, small games and toys, and "special friends." Older children can take their tape players and earphones, although they are not allowed to be used during takeoffs and landings.

There are certain precautions that should be taken when a child is traveling on his own. He should have his name, address, both parents' business and home telephone numbers and where he is going written down on one piece of paper to keep in a pocket and another to place in his luggage. To be on the safe side, a relative or friend's name and phone number could be on the list as well. He should have enough money in his wallet to make telephone calls and should know how to use a pay phone to make a collect call. He should also be knowledgeable about street-proofing skills. If there is a mixup at the terminal, you want to be sure that your child knows to whom he can go for help.

BUILDING A LIFE AS A SINGLE PERSON

There's a need to see my son and a need to have my own space. When he leaves for his mom's, I breathe a sigh of relief, and when he comes back, I'm really glad to see him. I use baby-sitters from time to time, but most of the time I just work around our schedule. One year I found out when the local ski club was having its get-togethers and switched weekends with my son's mother so that I could go. Then the ski club changed dates. You just have to live with this kind of stuff and laugh about it.

In retrospect, I think shared parenting is hardest on the parents. You've got a life that's a yo-yo. If you look at single people without kids, they have a certain life-style. There are people they see every weekend, they go out to lunch, they have a routine. But when I have my kids, they come first. Now that the kids are older I feel more comfortable about going out in the evening and leaving them with a baby-sitter. I just never wanted to before. Now I need to put my needs ahead of theirs a little bit more.

During the adjustment period after divorce, many parents feel lonely and disconnected from the world around them. Sometimes it is easier to concentrate solely on the role of mother or father than it is to venture out in the new role of single person. Worrying about your child and feeling that you must always be with her when she is living with you are common feelings. However, as time goes on, freeing those ties may be healthy for you both. It frees your child from feeling that she must take the place of the absent parent ("Daddy needs me. He's all alone.") and allows you to pursue your own needs for adult companionship and other interests outside home and the workplace.

Although baby-sitters can be expensive, relying on your coparent to help out on the evenings that you would like to go out is not a good idea. Coparents are often willing to oblige, but the disruption of the schedule is often confusing for a young child. The best arrangement is to use a caregiver who is already known to the child and used by both parents. If this isn't possible, because you have child-free evenings in a shared parenting plan, you are in a good position to be able to trade nights with a friend or to join a neighborhood baby-sitting co-op. In lieu of this arrangement, you should try to find one reliable baby-sitter. Ask friends or neighbors for recommendations or contact your local junior or senior high school. Some schools offer baby-sitting courses, as do groups such as St. John Ambulance.

After a separation, some people throw themselves into a career to fill the gap that is sometimes left in their personal lives. This can lead to career advancement and higher self-esteem but may prevent you from finding the time to rebuild your emotional and personal life.

Pursuing your own interests outside work and family means leaving the grieving process and the past behind and stepping into the present. In his book, *Creative Divorce*, divorce therapist Mel Krantzler describes the benefits of doing this: "To me, one of the most exciting consequences of coming to terms with the past is the freedom to strive for your own particular brand of well-being. A complete change of life-style is not required. One of the greatest rewards of living creatively in the present (as against existing passively, responding only to others' wishes and demands) is the freedom to savor each moment for the pleasure it may provide, to appreciate accustomed pastimes for themselves once again instead of as poor substitutes for an empty life, and to explore and expand the dimensions of the independent person you are becoming."

There will be parts of your old life that you will want to bring into your new life. Friends are one. Inevitably, though, some of the friends that a former couple had as "couple friends" will no longer be a part of either's network of friends after divorce. Friendships that are couple-based are the most likely ones to be weakened by separation. Some friends will be supportive of one spouse but not the other. And still others will try to be friendly with both former partners. Sometimes the latter group will assume that, because a couple has a shared parenting arrangement, they will have no problems socializing together at events held by mutual friends.

There was one set of friends who didn't want to choose sides, and that was fine except they would keep inviting us both to functions. I reached a point where I told my friend that I didn't want to go because I felt uncomfortable and I thought everyone else did too. She replied by accusing me of ruining her party by being selfish. So I said, "Well, someday if you go through this, you'll know exactly how I feel. I'm sorry but I'm not coming." At some point you have to take care of yourself. You can't be doing things because someone else thinks it's the proper thing to do.

When coparents belong to the same religious congregation, social group or club, it is often impossible for them both to continue attending. To avoid putting their friends and themselves in an awkward position, one person usually leaves to join another group somewhere else. Generally, the person who leaves is the one who has a wider circle of friends elsewhere and is in less need of support.

As parents pursue interests that they have always wanted to explore, new friends will enter their lives. Some people find it helpful to join single-parent groups at this time. Although there isn't a national group for parents with shared parenting arrangements, there are branches of Parents Without Partners, One Parent Families Association of Canada and other local single-parent support groups across Canada (see Resource List or contact your local family service association).

Reaching out to others and reaching within yourself can help open the door to a new life for you and your children. The less emotional baggage you take through that door, the more free you and your family will be to pursue the challenging, yet rewarding, life awaiting you.

Your Preschooler

6

The first year of our separation, I think our kids sensed how tense and unhappy their parents were. My preschooler was sensitive to that and it was a very hard year for him. He had a lot of interrupted sleep. Although it may be partly a normal stage of development, I'm convinced that his adjustment has to do with how well we all are doing now. I'm much happier and much stronger this year and I think his father is too.

The complete dependence of a preschooler on his parents makes their separation more devastating for this age group than any other. The people he loves most — his parents — are no longer living together, and his world seems to have turned upside-down. A pre-schooler's highly active imagination may produce a flood of terrifying events that could happen to him or to his mother and father. They'll disappear. He'll be lost. They'll send him away. He'll be blamed. Such fears may seem incomprehensible to an adult but are very real to a young child. After all, hasn't something previously unimaginable already happened to his family? The younger a child is, the more emotionally overwhelmed he may be by the changes in his life. A two-and-a-half- to three-and-a-half-year-old will have more difficulty comprehending these changes than a three-and-a-half- to five-year-old. With proper care, sensitivity and frequent contact with both parents, a preschooler of any age can be helped through this stressful time.

BREAKING THE NEWS

Telling your child that you and your partner are separating and helping him understand the reasons for it are probably the most difficult challenges that you will have to face as parents. It is particularly difficult when the child is a preschooler. An older child has some concept of what divorce is, but a three- to five-year-old has no understanding at all. This is why it is important to keep your explanation as simple as possible. One counselor draws the parallel of telling children about sex. Complex details about the reasons for your divorce, although important to you, are as bewildering and unimportant to your child as anatomical details are in response to the question "Where do babies come from?"

Childcare experts recommend that you tell your child about your separation together, at home and at least a week before one of you moves. The one thing that your child needs to know, and will need to be told over and over again, is that although his parents can no longer be happy living together as husband and wife, they will continue being his parents and will continue loving him. They will do this in two homes rather than one. Older preschoolers with some concept of time can be told about the time-sharing plan, while younger ones simply need to be reassured that they will see both parents often. Both need to know that their mother and father will continue feeding, clothing and playing with them as before. Using specific examples of how you will care for your child will be more easily understood than vague reassurances such as "Mommy and Daddy will still take care of you."

HELPING YOUR CHILD OVERCOME HER FEARS

My three-year-old was furious with me. She didn't want to go to my apartment and used to say over and over again, "I don't want to be with you." It made me feel terrible because I felt so guilty. When a child starts reacting that way, it brings up all those horrible doubts you have about your decision to separate. I tried not to let it get to me and to help her as best I could. There were times, though, when we would both stand there crying. But then you realize that you have to get on with your life. And gradually things start getting better for both of you.

Your child may react to the news of your separation immediately or not for several days. One reaction may be anger — toward the parent who is leaving, the one who is remaining or both. In a formerly even-tempered child, this rage can be especially upsetting for parent and preschooler. Each time a little fist beats against your body you may feel that it is deserved a hundredfold. And each time a little voice cries "I don't love you" or "I don't want to be with you," you may experience an overwhelming sense of guilt and shame. This is a true test of parenthood, of putting one's own hurt feelings on hold to reassure your child that you understand her feelings, that those feelings are OK, and that they will pass in time. Your own feelings of guilt are a healthy reaction to your child's pain. It is unlikely that they will ever completely disappear, but they can be reduced by protecting your preschooler from any further suffering caused by parental actions or words.

After our separation, in addition to being angry with his father and me from time to time, Mark had a desperate need to know where we were if he couldn't see us. At my house, after I had tucked him into bed at night and gone into the living room, we would do a voice check to assure him that he could hear me and that I could hear him. "Testing, one, two, three, can you hear me, Mark?" At his dad's, he didn't like David doing laundry in the basement while he was falling asleep. It was too far away. Sometimes he was afraid of becoming lost between the two houses.

This fear of abandonment is the most powerful negative feeling that preschoolers may experience after their parents separate. In shared parenting arrangements, young children are sometimes terrified that the parent who leaves will not return and that the parent who remains will go away. At this stage in their development, although preschoolers are beginning to learn to separate their own identity from that of their parents, they still see their parents as one person who looks after them, not as individuals. They have great difficulty imagining how the family will continue after the separation and how they will be cared for. "Will Daddy still be my daddy?" and "Who will take care of me?" are common questions.

Because children are also very self-centered at this age, they sometimes blame themselves for the changes that are taking place in their family. For example, a preschooler's normal attachment to the opposite-sex parent can promote feelings of responsibility if the same-sex parent leaves. In his unconscious mind, a child may believe that his wish to have his mother all to himself has magically come true. Similarly, when the opposite-sex parent moves, he may feel, as one little boy did, "If you love someone too much, they leave." A preschooler's sense of guilt can lead him to imagine that going from one home to another is a punishment for "wrong thoughts" or misbehavior, and this in turn may lead him to believe that his parents can divorce him too. Children need to be reassured that they are not to blame and that a parent's love for his or her child is a special kind of love that never ends. They need to know that their parents are unhappy with each other, not with them.

Unlike adults or older children, preschoolers don't have the skills to cope with all of this stress in what we would see as a positive way. They can't talk to friends, jog around the block or attend yoga classes. Their response to feelings of hurt and fear is often a return to an earlier behavior. Bedwetting, changes in sleep and diet patterns, reverting to baby talk and thumbsucking are some forms of this regressive behavior. Another sign of stress to watch for is the child who is too well behaved. If his parents are depressed and withdrawn much of the time, a child may feel threatened, try to be perfect in order not to disturb the parents further, and feel miserable when he fails.

There aren't any guaranteed methods of calming a preschooler's fears during this period of adjustment. Parents find that they rely on ways they have used in the past to comfort their child. Admittedly, Mommy and Daddy's not living together anymore doesn't compare with their leaving to go to a party, but the parenting skills used have some similarities. After acknowledging your child's pain and letting him know that you understand, you should trust your own instincts about what your child needs in the way of comforting, whether that is a cozy cuddle in an armchair, playing together with a favorite stuffed toy or reading a familiar story. Time spent alone with your child with no outside distractions may be the best way to reassure him of your love and concern.

Contrary to what some people might think, there is no research to show that children of this age benefit from being prompted to talk about their feelings. Constantly asking them what they are feeling about the separation, although well meaning, may distress rather than help them. On the other hand, if regressive or "too perfect" behavior occurs, psychiatrist Sol Goldstein in his book *Divorced Parenting: How to Make It Work*, suggests that a parent let his or her child know he or she is aware of the tension being felt and that it would be better for the child to express these feelings directly to the parent in words — or even in crying — than by such behavior. It's very important not to blame children for the behavior. They simply need encouragement to pick another way to express their feelings and a large amount of patience on your part.

Fathers, in particular, may feel inadequate or incapable of helping a screaming, distraught preschooler or one who is sad and withdrawn. Unfortunately, our society has not generally prepared men for a nurturing role. At first, a single father may feel inadequate when it comes to comforting or caring for his child, especially if he has played the second-parent role in the family. It takes time for some fathers to develop their own parenting style and the self-confidence to ask for help when they need it. Help is available through friends and family members who are parents, and in books, parenting magazines and childcare seminars given by various social agencies. In a good shared parenting arrangement, though, his coparent may be a father's best source of advice. A parenting plan that gradually increases the father's role in child raising may also be appropriate for those men who haven't shared the parenting in the marriage. Because studies have shown that a good father-child relationship is important to the self-esteem and psychological well-being of a child whose parents have divorced, the efforts of coparents to foster this relationship is well worthwhile.

I don't think I was a terrific caregiver in the beginning. There were a lot of things that threw me. I was pretty good at the mechanical details of changing the diapers and playing with my son, but when things were rocky, when he was screaming, I felt totally lost.

The biggest challenge for me was being loving and nurturing to my children. This kind of loving was foreign to me because I hadn't experienced it in my own family. My father loved us but he loved us in the way that many fathers love—from an enormous distance. He wasn't nurturing and he wasn't physical. We didn't hug or any of that kind of stuff. These were things I felt I believed in, but when it came time to do them, it was very difficult for me.

Together, a mother and father can help their preschooler overcome negative feelings about the changes in the family. It may take time, but parents can help their young child adapt to a shared parenting arrangement by listening to their child's troubles, reminding him physically as well as in words of their love, focusing on his strengths, protecting him as much as possible from exposure to parental conflict, and stressing the positive things about their new lives.

SETTING UP A NEW HOME FOR A PRESCHOOLER

The most humbling event of the whole move came when we'd finished moving into my new apartment. My son and I were in the elevator and another man got on with us. Ivor looked at him and asked, "Do you live here?" When the man said he did, Ivor got this knowing look on his face and said, "Oh, you must fight with your wife too." He thought that it was a place people came to when they'd fought with their wives. It was funny but it was really sad too.

It takes time for children to consider a second home their home rather than an adult place where Mom or Dad lives. They need to feel comfortable and secure before "your house" becomes "our house." Two ways to accomplish this are to childproof and child-decorate.

Childproofing allows you both to feel at ease in your new surroundings. Equipping sockets with dummy plugs, checking that screens on windows are safe, putting breakable objects out of reach, locking medicines and cleaning materials away — all mean that you don't have to be constantly telling your child not to do this or not to do that. Decorating with your child in mind serves the same purpose. There may be a temptation, in furnishing your new home, to buy that off-white rug or sofa that you've always wanted, but do you really want to stand guard over it for the next five years of your youngster's life? Other ways to make a preschooler feel at home include:

- Providing something familiar from his other bedroom in his new bedroom or a corner of your bedroom that will be his (for example, the same patterned sheets, the same wallpaper border print or same-colored blind or curtains);
- Buying an inexpensive frame or two and framing special pictures that he's given you for his bedroom or another place in the house or apartment;
- Taping his artwork up on the fridge;
- Buying or borrowing from the library some of his favorite bedtime stories and tapes;

- Reserving the bottom shelf of a bookcase for his books and toys;
- Getting him a library card with his new address on it;
- Buying something special for the house or apartment together (mugs, eggcups, glasses), one for him and one for you.

Before your child comes to see his new home for the first time, it's also a good idea to pick up some of the basic preschooler playthings — a set of blocks, a ball, playdough, art supplies. This indicates that you've been thinking about him as you've been setting up your new home and gives you something to do together after your initial exploration of the house or apartment.

You will probably find that, unlike the family possessions, your preschooler's toys will not be evenly divided between the two homes. Parents who have been able to keep the family home for a time are often reluctant to upset their child's environment any more than is necessary, so the parent who is leaving will often take some of the more unpopular toys but leave the rest. A new set of toys can be built up inexpensively over time by picking through yard sales, browsing in secondhand stores and collecting hand-me-downs from friends and family. (Our first sandbox — an old plastic wading pool — was found in a neighbor's garbage.) At this age, children will be just as delighted with cardboard moving boxes and tubes, old dress-up clothes and collections of odd buttons as they will be with new, "bought" toys.

One word of warning, though. It takes time for preschoolers to learn to share their possessions with other children. This is particularly true of a child whose world has been shattered and who may be desperately holding on to what remains. His need to possess should be respected.

When another child is coming to visit, special toys can be put away and the visiting parent asked to bring toys from his or her home. As a child becomes more comfortable with his new world, he will become more open to the concept of sharing.

In addition to playing with toys, preschoolers love exploring and helping. The home you move into is unlikely to be the one of your dreams, but it is something new for your child to discover and help you with and, as such, can pick up his spirits after the separation. To make the introduction to a second home as unstressful an experience as possible, parents should take advantage of this natural curiosity and willingness to help. Can your child sort his toys into bins or boxes? Water plants for you? Help decide where to put his books? Being optimistic about your new home and involving your child in setting it up go a long way to injecting something positive into unhappy times.

LIVING IN TWO HOMES

There are many steps that parents can take to help their children adjust to their new way of life, although it is important to keep in mind that, even when these steps are taken, it may take a year or more, depending on age and temperament, for a preschooler to feel truly comfortable living in two homes. Missing the absent parent is one major source of distress. This is common to every age group, but the sorrow it causes in a preschooler is truly heartrending, simply because it is often so hard to convince her that the other parent loves her and will see her again. Eventually, as the absent parent appears as you said he or she would, the child will lose her fear of abandonment and will be less clingy. However, in the meantime, you can reassure her by making transitions from one home to the other as easy as possible and by helping your child understand when she will see each parent.

Before a changeover, coparents usually give preschoolers plenty of advance notice, coupled with reassurance. If you are making transitions directly, the best way to help is by keeping your battles out of the hallway and away from your child. Parental hostility makes transfers difficult for this age group. Even when you both are doing your best to be calm and cheerful, you should expect some negative reactions before, during and after changeovers. A tantrum, for example, doesn't reflect on the parenting ability of your coparent but is a normal reaction to a scary situation.

Your child's "cuddlies" can be an enormous comfort to her at these times. This definitely isn't the time to decide that a blanket or soother has been outgrown, or to react negatively if she returns to a security aid after giving it up. She needs every comforting thing in her life right now and every effort should be made to accommodate that need, even if it means making a special trip to retrieve a favorite that has been left behind.

Siblings are another source of support. Many sisters and brothers who go through the divorce process together tend to look out for one another. Even children as young as four or five can be attentive to a sibling's needs. Later on, parents may want to have the children's changeover days at different times so that they can spend time alone with each child, but it isn't recommended at this age.

I think children do adjust as long as they're loved and they have some consistency in their lives and they have each other, which is a very strong bond. Eight years ago, when my sons were two and four, they went back and forth together and they still do.

Some parents suggest getting preschoolers actively

involved in the transfer. After choosing their own back-pack, they can be taught to pack their cuddlies and toys in it before each move. This gives them a measure of control over the event. Depending upon their age, children can also be taught to use the telephone. Allowing them to phone their other parent after arriving at their second home reassures them that he or she is still "back there."

To help Mark understand when he was going to be with me and when he was going to be with his father, we made a calendar together. David's days were marked with circles with mustaches; mine were marked with circles with curly hair. The calendar was only for a month at a time and was taped to the refrigerator door. It was something positive that we could do together and, as we worked on it, it gave Mark an opportunity to talk about the separation if he felt like it. It was also something concrete, something he could see. He could see that there were a lot of Daddy faces and a lot of Mummy faces and could check off the days until he saw each of us. Other parents have used different colors for each parent. Some people use plastic sorting boxes for younger preschoolers. If there are three days between transfers, they put three blocks in one box and each morning the child puts a block into the sorting box.

The predictability of the schedule is very important for this age group. Children feel secure knowing what to expect at any one time. Changing schedules strictly for convenience because "something has come up" is hard for them to handle. This is why coparents of preschoolers often go out on the days they don't have the children with them rather than use baby-sitters. If you do want to go away for a vacation on your own, counselors suggest that one week is the maximum amount of time you should not be in contact with a child of this age. Telephoning frequently is advisable. One ardent camper I know came up with two ways to let her preschooler know that she was thinking of him while she was off in the wilds for several days and could not telephone. On one occasion she made a tape of herself reading his favorite stories and singing their special songs so that he could play it whenever he needed to hear her voice. When he was a little older, she wrote a note for his father to read to him each day she would be away and included a small surprise in each one. These are simple suggestions, but they provide reassurance to worried preschoolers.

In your day-to-day living, you can help a preschooler feel more secure by following similar routines in each home. Toilet training is one example. It's a good idea to each have the same book on the subject and follow the same philosophy, and to use a similar potty chair or adapter seat. Because bedtimes are often problematic at this age anyway, many parents also try to follow the same bedtime routine. However, the routine on its own won't necessarily prevent a preschooler from being afraid to go to sleep at night.

Being frightened at night is often tied in to a young child's fear of abandonment. When you, yourself, are lonely and feeling guilty about your child's being upset, it is easy to fall into a pattern of sleeping with him. One parent who allowed his son to sleep with him found that, although his child was comforted and his own guilt feelings were allayed, his son's thrashing around in the bed kept him awake most of the night. In the morning, the father was grumpy and impatient with his son, the comfort of the night before in effect being wiped out by his inability to cope the next day. To help his child feel more comfortable in his own bed, the father equipped the room with a nightlight, left the bedroom door open, gave his son as many hugs and assurances as were needed to comfort him and told him that he would return to check in on him before going to bed.

Nightmares are another bedtime problem. Although they may indicate that a child is having difficulty coping with his parents' separation and his new life, they are a normal occurrence at this age. Waking up alone after a nightmare is terrifying for preschoolers, so it is important to get to them as quickly as possible after you hear them cry out. If you are a heavy sleeper and depended in the past on your mate to hear your child, an intercom might be a wise investment.

Because there are so many changes in the preschool years, so much to be taught and so much to be learned, coparents must communicate with each other. When a new skill is learned or an old routine discarded, it helps to jot it down to give to the other parent. This avoids frustration on all sides — "But I just got rid of his pacifier! Why did you buy him a new one?" In some cases, it is letting your child learn by doing that needs to be communicated — "I'm not putting his shoes on any longer. What about you?"

Being overly helpful and protective is a common pitfall of divorced parents. As a preschooler, my little guy would try something once and if it didn't work, it seemed like the end of the world. He let us know that we would have to put his socks on for him until he was twenty, because he would never be able to do it himself. When you feel you've caused your child so much pain already, it's very easy to fall into the habit of sparing him any more frustration or sadness by doing everything for him. It also makes life simpler for you when you're trying to rush out the door to get to work on time. In the end, though, it doesn't help the child or the parent. What a preschooler whose parents have separated needs is a giant dose of self-confidence, and one way to get it is by learning to do things for himself. By helping him be independent now, you are also paving the way for a successful group day-care or school experience.

DAY CARE

Kristin and her father and I were all at a Christmas party at the day care and afterward one of the day care workers said that she really found it a pleasure to be around us because everything was always so amicable. She then told us about a couple whose son had attended the center. They were separated and refused to be in the same place at the same time. So if one of them happened to be at the day care and the other one dropped in, he or she would go rushing out without even saying hello. It was very stressful for the child, who would start crying. He felt a lot of tension in this type of situation and of course everyone else did too. I couldn't put my child through that, no matter what my feelings were for my former spouse.

Most parents with preschoolers in day care try to continue the arrangement they had before the separation. If your child attends a day-care center, the staff will likely have had experience with children whose parents have separated; however, they may not have had experience helping children adjust to a shared parenting arrangement. It is necessary to explain your time-sharing plan with them, and you may also want to give them some information on the topic of shared parenting. If you have a caregiver, she may not have experience with a child whose parents are separating. For this reason, it is even more important to acquaint her with the changes in your family and to provide her with ways to explain those changes to your child in a positive and reassuring way.

If one of you has been home with your child and will now be re-entering the work force, you have some decisions to make about day care. Ideally, you should start your child in day care before you separate in order to prevent her from having to adjust not only to the separation but also to the loss of her primary caregiver.

Your day-care choices include the following, although some are more readily available than others: licensed day-care centers that provide group care, licensed and unlicensed family day care, which also provides group care but in the caregiver's home, workplace day care, and a nanny or caregiver who looks after your child in your own and/or your coparent's home. There are advantages and disadvantages to each one; however, research has shown that, in general, children show no ill effects if the day care is high quality. For children of divorce, in addition to the quality of care, consistent care is an important factor to keep in mind. If you are considering a day-care center, one with low staff turnover is preferable.

Some coparents have been able to find a caregiver who is willing to follow their time-sharing schedule and come to both homes to care for their child. If you decide to follow this route, you will need to hire someone who is flexible — able to follow different directions in two homes — and confidential, that is, able to resist the temptation to carry tales back and forth. It is a good idea to draw up a letter outlining his or her duties: hours of work at each home, vacation times, childcare responsibilities, housekeeping duties, who to contact in case of emergency, fees and deductions (you must deduct taxes, workers' compensation, UIC and CPP; Revenue Canada can provide directions).

Information on selecting day care can be obtained by writing to the National Childcare Information Centre, Health and Welfare Canada, Sixth Floor, Brooke-Claxton Building, Ottawa, Ontario K1A 1B5. You might also want to consult a Canadian book entitled *Child Care: Options for Working Parents* by Janet Rosenstock and Eva M. Rosenstock, or the section on day care in *The Canadian Parents' Sourcebook* by Ellen Roseman and Colleen Darragh.

STARTING SCHOOL

While other teachers' names and faces fade over the years, many people remember their kindergarten teacher; most fondly, a few disparagingly. She often was the first adult outside the family circle to care for us for a consistent length of time each day. Today, the majority of children are in day care and many have a number of nonfamily caregivers; however, their first schoolteacher is still special. For a child of divorce, this is especially true. A kindergarten teacher can provide continuity, affection and support in a jumbled-up world.

If your child has not yet started school, and you have a choice of kindergarten teachers, it is wise to meet the teachers before classes begin. Schools often have open houses for parents of new students, or you can simply ask the principal to arrange classroom visits for you. By observing the class, you will be able to tell which teacher would best suit your child's needs. A rocking chair for cuddles is always a good sign, as is a warm personality rather than a no-nonsense one. Be sure to check if the teacher is frequently sick (you can ask neighborhood parents), if a retirement is imminent (some school boards allow teachers to retire midyear) or if a half-year sabbatical is planned. Your child needs a consistent, reassuring presence at this time, not a succession of supply teachers.

WHEN YOUR CHILD IS ILL

The children's father doesn't believe in medicine at all, not even painkillers, and I believe in some medication and antibiotics. We've had quite a bit of conflict over this and it's tough because there's no compromise.

If one of the children was sick and wanted the other parent, well, why not? I would phone and say she's sick and has been asking for you, and sometimes we could change our schedules and sometimes we couldn't. We respected their feelings and tried not to see it as game-playing or manipulation.

What to do when your preschooler is ill needs to be discussed before it happens, particularly if you and your coparent have different views on the subject. Your child doesn't need the added stress of battling parents when he's under the weather. On changeover days when a child is sick, coparents sometimes choose to have the child stay with the parent he is with.

Some mothers and fathers attend doctor's appointments together. At this age, when there tends to be a more frequent time-sharing schedule, having both parents at the doctor's office can help to fill in the gaps about the progress of an illness. However, if the visit turns into a time to blame the other parent for the illness, the plus turns into a minus. Most coparents simply try to communicate with each other as much as possible when their child is sick, rather than attend appointments together.

Entrusting your coparent with a sick child at this age can be trying for some parents. Knowing that your coparent has all the necessary equipment, books and doctors' phone numbers helps, as does the assurance that your phone calls are accepted as concern for your child rather than distrust of your coparent's abilities to care for a sick son or daughter.

INFANTS AND TODDLERS

The advantage of separating when children are very young is that they never know anything different. My marriage ended when my son was a baby. He's ten now and one of his friends, whose parents separated when he was four, still wants them to get back together. Justin likes it this way.

Although there may be a future advantage to sharing custody of an infant or toddler, being coparents of a child in this age group requires great care, planning and cooperation. Little research has been carried out on shared parenting of very young children. However, childcare professionals generally agree that before the age of three, most children need the stability of one home. In most cases, the primary caregiver's home serves as the child's main residence with the other parent visiting frequently and caring for the child on a preplanned schedule. During the early years, short periods away from the mother can be expanded into longer periods at the father's home. Depending upon the reaction of the child, overnight stays can begin at the age of three or even younger, although entire weekends may still be too long a time away from the home base.

As with the reactions of all children to their parents' separation, those of infants and toddlers will vary. Even babies will sense that their parents are tense and may react by crying more. Toddlers may regress, behave aggressively with peers or be excessively clingy. All are normal reactions that will change as you help your child adapt to his new life.

Consistency of care, familiar routines and the attention of two loving parents are essential for a child of this age. Both parents should become familiar with the developmental changes of early childhood (Penelope Leach's *Your Baby and Child* is a well-known favorite) so they can spot behavior that is not part of a normal developmental phase and, hence, requires attention. If both parents have returned to work, it is very important to have the same caregiver for the first few years of a child's life. In a day-care situation parents can ask that one person be assigned to look after their child so that he can develop a one-to-one relationship with that person.

Your School-Age Child

7

I like having two homes because you get to see both your parents a lot and you never get bored.

Whenever I'm at Dad's, I start to miss Mom and whenever I'm at Mom's I start to miss Dad. It's nice to talk to them on the phone or to meet them for lunch or something.

Researchers have found that school-age children may be able to adapt to shared parenting more easily than preschoolers. Children of this age can make their feelings known verbally, can handle transitions and changes in routines, are more independent and are less likely to feel rejected by their parents. In *Second Chances*, researcher Judith Wallerstein writes that "six-to-ten-year-olds may even enjoy the sense of being courted by two parents, of dividing their favors and holidays." However, it's wise to keep in mind that shared parenting does not protect a child from the initial distress of divorce. Older children go through the grieving process just as preschoolers do.

BREAKING THE NEWS

After a definite decision to separate has been made, family counselors suggest that a child be told, if possible, by both parents together, at home, and preferably on a weekend. When parents are comfortable with the idea of telling their child together, they sometimes take turns explaining the reasons for the separation so that the child knows that it is a mutual decision and that neither parent is to blame. Attaching blame forces a youngster to feel that he must choose sides. Not giving reasons for the separation may lead a child to blame himself.

Honest, basic reasons appropriate to the age of the child are best. They help prevent a loss of trust that is the unhappy result when parental lies are uncovered later in life. It is wiser to tell a child that one parent doesn't love the other parent and is in love with someone else than to chance a relative telling the child a few years later. Simply stated reasons also help prevent further uncertainty in a child's mind during an uncertain time. For example, presenting the news with happy faces and general good cheer confuses a child and makes him wonder what worse news his parents might be hiding. Talk of "this might only be temporary," gives a child false hope, which prevents him from grieving and then continuing on with his life. Honest discussion rather than sugarcoated or false information allows a child to work through what is happening to him and why.

Letting your son or daughter know what won't change may be as important as discussing what will. There is usually something that will remain constant in your child's life after the separation. Friends? Activities? School? All are vital parts of a child's world. It will comfort him to know that not all areas of his life will be affected by his parents' separation. Most important, he needs to be told that the love adults feel for each other may change, but the love parents feel for their children never does.

When discussing the shared parenting arrangement,

children should probably not be asked their opinion of the time-sharing arrangement or given choices at this time. Faced with the devastating news of their parents' separation, they are ill-equipped to make decisions. Changes may be requested by children at a later date and accommodated, but beginning shared parenting with one plan and trying it out for awhile is recommended. Questions about the separation and the parenting plan should be answered simply, avoiding detail that might confuse or frustrate. If a child wants to know more, he will ask.

Although some parents tell siblings separately because of their age differences, many counselors believe that the family should be told together so there is no confusion or anger over why one child is given special treatment by being taken aside to be told something. Brothers and sisters also need one another's support during this painful time. Elder siblings can be given more details later.

A child's immediate reactions to the news of his parents' separation may include sobbing, pleading, anger, fear, false bravado or denial. Seeming indifference may be replaced by tears hours or days later. Tears may be replaced by anger. Whatever the reactions are, it is important to allow a child to express his emotions fully. Parents can help by encouraging their child to talk about his hurt and anger. They can let him know that these are normal feelings, that they understand, and that the feelings will pass in time. Above all, a school-age child needs to know that both parents will always love him and that there will be happier times ahead for all of you.

Parents with shared parenting arrangements sometimes assume that, because their child sees both parents on a regular basis, he should be happier than a child of a traditional divorce. They point out that Lila only sees her dad every other weekend, or that Sam's mom lives across the country and he only sees her on holidays. This type of argument doesn't help children who are grieving, who need to be allowed to feel unhappy about their parents' separation. Most children recognize this type of talk for what it is — an attempt by adults to make them feel better. But it doesn't really make them feel better. Later they may see shared parenting as evidence of their parents' ongoing commitment and love for them. And eventually, many children in shared parenting arrangements say that they prefer their parents' parenting plan to other plans. In the beginning, though, they feel very sad and very unlucky.

Parents may also assume that, because their marriage has been marked by heated arguments, their children will be as relieved that they are separating as they themselves may be. However, very few children are actually relieved when they are told that their parents are separating.

After a year or more, when younger children hear that their parents are going to get a divorce, they may become upset all over again. While their parents are separated, they tend to believe there is a chance the family could be reunited. Divorce seems very final to them.

A SCHOOLCHILD'S FEARS

Our children didn't have that much difficulty with the separation. In fact, I think in our minds it was more of an issue to have it talked about and worked through than for them. More often the response I got was "Leave me alone. I'm OK. You always try to make me talk about it."

In the adjustment period after divorce, some children

do adapt more easily than others. Even the reactions of siblings may be markedly different. Some of a school-child's reactions may parallel the preschooler's: diet and sleep disruption, regression, "acting out" behavior, feeling they are to blame, sadness and anger. Children as old as age seven may also experience abandonment fears.

While six- to eight-year-olds often react with sadness, nine- to twelve-year-olds more often react with anger. The anger stems from a sense of betrayal by their parents and an overwhelming sense of powerlessness in the face of that betrayal. Anger should be accepted by parents as part of the mourning process and not reacted to with disapproval or hurt.

Loyalty conflict can be especially destructive for some children in this age group. Children will remember, even into adulthood, the pressure of having to side with one parent over another and being dragged into parental squabbles. A tendency toward seeing situations as all black or all white makes nine- to twelve-year-olds highly vulnerable to the accusations of one parent against the other. Parents who want their child to feel the same way about their former partner as they do are disregarding their child's needs to have a continuing relationship with both parents. For a child to be able to do this, he must know that each parent believes it is fine for him to love the other parent and that both are glad that he does.

Reunification fantasies are also common in this age group and may last for years. Three years after his parents' divorce, one little boy confided to his mother that, if he had his wish, his dad, mom and his favorite stepsister would live in one house and his stepfather, stepmother and other stepsister would live in another house. Sometimes school-age children will get into trouble because they know this will force their parents to come together to solve the problem. Counselors recommend that parents impress on their children from the start that the separation is final and, just as nothing they ever did caused the separation, nothing they could do in the future would reunite their parents. You should not brutally strip children of their fantasies, but instead gently help them differentiate between fantasy and reality.

Some children act out the conflict they feel with aggressive behavior, while others direct the conflict inward. In the latter group, physical symptoms may appear — headaches, stomachaches or vague complaints of "feeling sick." These physical complaints are more common in children under ten than in older children.

This list of possible reactions may seem daunting. It's important to realize that not every child will experience all of these reactions. Being forewarned simply allows you to be ready as a parent to comfort and help your child.

How can you help? First, by reassuring your child again and again, verbally and physically, that you love him and will continue to take care of him. Second, by listening and paying attention to his concerns and encouraging him to express his feelings and to ask questions. Some parents have found family meetings helpful, with each parent meeting with the children. Child psychiatrist Rudolf Dreikurs, author of *Children: The Challenge*, recommends that these be held on a regular basis. Children are asked to begin the discussion so that the meeting isn't seen as a forum for the parent to present problems and offer solutions. Finding solutions to problems as a family may prevent children from feeling alone and isolated.

During the time that you aren't with your children, especially during the adjustment period, a telephone call will reassure children that you still care. One parent recommends that you don't wait for your child to call.

Although your child should be told that he can call you at any time, it shouldn't be his responsibility to make the contact. Many newly separated parents aren't used to talking to their child on the phone and may be disconcerted at the reception their calls receive. The attention span of younger children can be limited, and when they are absorbed in play they will tell you. You often wind up feeling like you're playing second fiddle to Barbie or a Ninja Turtle. When this happens, it's easy to wonder whether it's worth calling; however, the very fact that you called is what matters to your child, not the length or substance of the conversation. One last pointer from a seasoned coparent: "A month after the separation, I called my daughter when a friend was in the room. My friend told me that my voice was about as downbeat as it could be. It sounded like I was ready to jump off a bridge. I realized that my daughter would worry excessively about me if she thought I was lonely, so after that when I called, I tried to sound upbeat and talked about what I was doing instead of just asking her questions about what she was doing."

Books are another way to help children cope during this period. Young readers who identify with the lead character in a book feel more comfortable discussing their problems. It is important, though, to choose a book that truly matches the child's situation and to discuss how the book relates to the child. Books for children of divorce are listed on page 212.

PROBLEMS LATER ON

He has his problems, but who doesn't? He seems to be going through a very normal period for eleven-year-olds. Being eleven is being a jerk, but I don't think his jerkiness has anything to do with shared parenting. He's bright, he doesn't seem to have any emotional problems, he likes his parents — he's very fond of all four of them!

When our children are toddlers, we often attribute certain behavioral traits, especially negative ones, to the age of the child. Remember the terrible twos? But by the time our youngsters are in school, most of us tend to be more confident in our parenting skills and don't refer to the experts as often. This is why, I think, we forget that every stage has its age-related problems, and why, when we separate or divorce, we tend to blame all of our children's later problems on the separation rather than considering that some of them may be related to age. This may be especially true of parents with one child, whose sole focus is on that child.

DEVELOPMENTAL CHARACTERISTICS OF
SCHOOL-AGE CHILDREN
When problems crop up months or even years after the separation, it might be helpful to consider the developmental stage your child is at before jumping to the conclusion that the divorce is the cause of the behavior. The following are some characteristics that you may notice in your child:

Six
- Compared with first stage of adolescence
- May be demanding, negative, subject to mood swings
- Conflict with mother is usual as child attempts to break away from her to enter larger world of school and friends
- Easily distracted
- Must cope with pressures and demands of Grade One and may be overtired at end of day

150

- Doesn't handle losing well
- Nightmares and new fears are common due to perceived high expectations of parents and partial knowledge of the world around him or her

Seven
- An introspective, more cooperative, less active age
- May seem withdrawn at times or self-absorbed
- Sensitive to criticism

Eight
- Active, less inward-looking
- Tends to be impatient
- Seems unmoved by scoldings, although will burst into tears when overtired
- Playing with one special friend is important

Nine
- Demands to be treated like a grown-up but sometimes reverts to behavior of a younger child
- Self-sufficient and self-motivated
- Important not to be different from friends

Ten
- A calm, tolerant, generally positive age
- Anger directed more often toward younger siblings than parents

Eleven
- Preadolescence begins; search for self-identity
- Self-assertive, argumentative, often disagreeable
- Subject to violent mood swings
- Anger directed toward parents and siblings
- Friendships have their ups and downs

- School performance may be erratic due to fatigue caused by emotional and body changes

Twelve
- More even-tempered than eleven
- Sometimes has periods of great fatigue when needs to be alone
- Anxious to be like peers
- May have pressure of moving from elementary school to junior high

One problem that parents do, in fact, help create is manipulativeness, which may develop in a child whose parents constantly compete for their child's affection. It is not unusual for a child to have a closer relationship with one parent than the other. This may have caused the other parent to feel a few twinges of envy when the family was together, but can turn into a worrisome jealousy when the couple separate. The jealousy in turn may lead to a destructive game of attempting to fulfill the child's every wish. This has nothing to do with the child—and children sense this, sometimes using their new-found power to manipulate both parents. Counselors advise that the best solution to this problem is simply not to play the game.

There may be times, however, directly after the separation or later, when parents don't feel that they can find a solution to their child's problems. If you sense that your child is in difficulty and needs help, there are many options available (see page 93). Talking to someone outside the family allows a child to express her feelings of pain without having to worry about their causing distress for the person listening.

There was a very sad time when our son was six. We were cuddling at bedtime and he burst into tears and said, "I feel as if you're pulling me in half; my daddy's got one leg and you've got the other and you're just pulling me in half." His father and I spent some time trying to figure out what we could do to make his life a little less divided, to try to glue the two pieces together more. We both shifted a bit on diet. I'm a heavy-duty health food vegetarian and his father provides a pretty straightforward North American diet, so we both bent some on that. We coordinated bedtimes. We coordinated what kind of chores were expected of him. We just tried to bring things a little bit more together. We also got him a therapist we both trusted, so he has an adult to whom he can begin to talk freely about what his struggles are.

SETTING UP A HOME FOR A SCHOOLCHILD

Establishing a second home for a schoolchild involves many of the same steps involved in setting one up for a preschooler (see page 129). To feel comfortable in a new home, a child must come to believe that he belongs there, that a bedroom or a corner of a bedroom is his and his alone, and that in the rest of the home he is welcome.

Some children are exposed to apartment life for the first time after a divorce. If you are moving into an apartment, instead of concentrating on the negative aspects—less space, no backyard—try to emphasize the positive. For example, they won't be expected to help in the garden or shovel snow, and there may be a community center close by, or other children in the building. Getting your children involved in decorating and asking for their suggestions is a better way to begin a new life than apologizing for the apartment or comparing it to what you've left.

If you are tight for space in your new apartment, here are some suggestions:

■ Store a large piece of plywood beside the refrigerator

or in a closet to place over the bathtub to create a crafts area or use a plastic tablecloth on the floor or over a table.

- Use the wall space by putting up shelving, bulletin boards, pegboards for holding toys and tools, and hooks for clothes.
- Toys, sports equipment and out-of-season clothes can be placed in storage bins under beds; board games and puzzles can be stored under the couch (how often do you clean under there anyway?).
- If you're buying a junior bed, consider one that has built-in storage drawers.

Setting up routines in a new home is another way to help a child feel secure and settled. Chores are a good example. Helping around the apartment or house makes children feel that they are an important part of a family, not just visitors who are with you every other week or whatever your time-sharing arrangement is. The chores don't have to be the same in each home; in fact, it's more interesting for the child if they are different. Letting children choose the chores they want to do prevents the "I don' wanna" routine and lets them feel more in control. Some parents may believe that their children have been through enough without expecting them to do housework too. However, chores also teach your child how to be self-sufficient. Try not to think of them as another burden your child has to bear, but as life skills.

SETTING LIMITS

My older daughter was very rule-conscious. I think she ordered her sister's and her world in a way to make it safer or easier to manage. They were quite happy to have rules. If they didn't get them from outside, they established their own.

If there is a problem, we are very good at talking it over on the phone to determine a united strategy. When we don't agree on what to do, we often have to hash it out until we can find something we agree on, or sometimes my ex gives in just so we're united.

Feeling guilty about the separation's effect on his or her child can interfere with a parent's enforcement of rules. A parent may tend to be overly permissive about things that wouldn't have been tolerated in the marriage. This can confuse a child. After divorce, children benefit from the security of knowing that their parents still care enough to make wise decisions on their behalf.

Most schoolchildren can adapt to different rules in different homes. Going to school, extracurricular activities and friends' homes have exposed them to the concept. Families may run into difficulty, however, when a child tries to enlist the help of a parent in changing a rule at her other home. When this happens, a child should be firmly told that, although you understand this is upsetting her, it is up to her to discuss the problem with the other parent.

Another pitfall to avoid in shared parenting is disciplining a child twice for the same behavior. One preteen treated flutes as if they were recyclable. In one week he managed to lose two of them. After the first one was lost, his father laid down the law, but it was a bad week for the boy and he left the new flute on the bus on his way to his mother's. Fortunately, it was found in the transit company's lost and found department. Because his mother had also impressed upon her son the consequences if he were to lose another flute, she saw little point in informing her coparent of the second loss, particularly since the lost item had been found.

CHILDREN LOOKING AFTER THEMSELVES

Contrary to popular belief, most "latchkey" children are not from single-parent families. There are times, however, when single parents are unable to provide parental care during all out-of-school hours. Generally speaking, a child under twelve should only be left alone if she possesses certain skills.

Cynthia Cole and Hyman Rodman, two American researchers, published a study in *Family Relations* on school-age children caring for themselves. Their guidelines for parents to use to judge their child's readiness for self-care include the following. The child should be able to:

- Physically control her body to avoid injury;
- Open locks and doors;
- Operate safely any accessible household equipment;
- Stay alone without much fear or loneliness;
- Deal with unexpected situations without excessive upset;
- Follow rules without testing them;
- Get help from friends and neighbors when needed;
- Understand the role of the fire and police departments and be willing to call when necessary;
- Maintain friendships with other children and adults.

In addition, the child should be capable of understanding and remembering verbal and written instructions, finding solutions to problems in a rational way and reading and writing well enough to take telephone and other messages. They recommend that parents or another adult be available by phone and for emergencies, and that the community be perceived as safe by all family members. Some Canadian communities have telephone numbers for children who are home alone and want to talk to an adult. Your community information center or family service association will be able to give you the number.

WHAT YOU CAN DO TO HELP YOUR CHILD AT SCHOOL

He started at a Catholic school with a small enrollment, and he was definitely the odd boy out. I know that, early on, he suffered a bit from it. The teacher noticed him daydreaming in class. Some of his behavior came from being different and being upset about it. He's overcome that. The way we've helped him is to attend school events together. That reinforces that we're both on his side.

It is only in the past decade that school administrators and teachers have awakened to the fact that a large percentage of students have parents who are divorced or separated. It's estimated that forty percent of all Canadian children will live in single-parent homes before the age of eighteen. Because sole-custody households are more common, coparents may find they must educate the educators on shared parenting.

If your decision to separate is made during the school year, your child's principal and teacher should be informed as soon as possible. They will need to know the kind of parenting plan you have worked out, what the transition day is, address changes, and how you plan to handle parent/teacher interviews. (You might want to consider attending interviews together. In some areas teachers are not paid extra for the parent/teacher interviews that take

157

place after school hours and may be resentful if they must hold two different meetings.) Some parents request separate notices. However, when there is cooperation between the parents, and a copying machine handy, it's a good idea to copy the important notices yourself. First of all, not all are of interest and, secondly, your child may not want to be the only kid receiving double sets of notices, especially in the beginning before he has adjusted to having two homes. Because progress reports may be sent home only two or three times a year, ask to be kept informed of your child's behavior in class and how it is affecting academic progress. If you have an alternate week, or split week, arrangement, the school should have your schedule and know which parent to call if the child becomes ill or is hurt.

When your child returns to school after the separation, his studies may suffer at first. His mind is on his troubles at home, and he may find it difficult to concentrate on reading, writing and arithmetic. If his sleep patterns have changed, he may be tired on top of it all. Because of this, both parents should set realistic goals for their child during the year after their marriage ends. They should also do everything they can to boost their child's self-esteem, which may have taken a nose-dive. Dr. Sol Goldstein writes in *Divorced Parenting* that one reason for a schoolchild's low self-esteem is his fear of being seen as different by his peers and teachers. He must be assured that his parents have discussed the situation with his teacher and that his schoolmates are unlikely to treat him any differently unless his fears cause him to act in a negative way.

As the adjustment period passes, some children try to turn their "difference" to their advantage. One girl got into trouble at school and was asked by her father how she could have handled the situation differently. Her reply was, "I should have told them I come from a broken home." Most teachers simply ignore the poor-little-victim game and the child stops playing it when she learns that it doesn't work. Other children try to use their two homes as an excuse for not doing homework — "I left it at my dad's house." Communication between parents is important when it comes to homework, particularly if a child needs a nudge from time to time. Assignments that are given in one parent's week and are due the next can easily fall between the homes unless an effort is made to warn the other parent.

In some schools, parents have helped form support groups for their children. For example, one group of parents was instrumental in helping to set up a pilot project for students of divorced or separated parents. The program has three different components: a ten-week discussion group for children, a support group for parents and an orientation session for teachers. It has run in two elementary schools thus far and is scheduled to run in two secondary schools. The groups are led by two social workers who are employed by, and are accountable to, the school board.

The group was criticized for taking the social workers away from their regular duties. Unfortunately, some principals tend to be reactive in their management skills. Instead of setting up preventive programs such as this one, their thinking tends to be crisis-oriented. Taking away a social worker from crisis management to set up a preventive program is foreign to many of them. However, bringing in outside social workers can also be a problem, because of the issue of territoriality — the school's social worker might feel left out of the process. Beyond a great deal of cooperation at all levels, to set up a group you will need: a professional leader who is accountable to the board, not simply someone who may like kids and has taken a few family-life courses; signed parental consent forms; time after school or at lunch hour; and someone to coordinate the schedule.

Other ways that you can help your child at school include:

- Ensuring there are library materials that include the experiences of children in all types of families;
- Discussing with the teacher the use of curriculum material that uses some alternatives to the nuclear, intact family as the only model of "family";
- In the junior grades, asking if "feeling" words (frustrated, jealous, annoyed, lonely, etc.) are being taught to help children express their emotions;
- If necessary, asking teachers to consider using more positive terms to describe one-parent families than "broken homes."

Finally, you know your child best. Be confident in the parenting plan that you have chosen for him and be wary of educators who question it. They know less about your situation than you do.

There were some concerns raised by our son's kindergarten teacher about whether joint custody was a reasonable arrangement. When he started kindergarten a year after the separation, he had a bit of a rough time. But we found that he had a rough time at the beginning of every year and still does to some extent; it's getting to know the kids in his class and getting comfortable with the teacher and all the rest of it. Then he settles down and turns into a great student. I don't think it has anything to do with the joint custody. He's just that kind of kid.

THE IMPORTANCE OF FRIENDS AND ACTIVITIES

Most of my friends have both of my numbers. I have one friend who has to walk about two minutes to get to my mom's, but he has to take a bus for about twenty minutes to visit when I'm at my dad's.

One way that you can provide continuity in your child's life is to try to ensure that she is able to maintain her friendships. Some counselors believe that this is especially true for seven- to twelve-year-olds. It helps to keep the child in the same school as before the separation and, if possible, to maintain a close proximity of residences.

Whether the child has attended a local school or has been bused to an out-of-district school in the past may make a difference in her friendship patterns. Those who are in neighborhoods where children are regularly bused to programs outside their district are accustomed to having friends at school and friends on their street or in their apartment building. Those who are in a local school tend to play with schoolmates who live close by. The child who may be at a disadvantage in shared parenting is the one who is allowed to continue going to the same school but whose parents have both moved out of the district.

Friendships made at extracurricular activities are also important to a child, as are the activities themselves. When told of their parents' decision to separate, many children are worried that they won't be able to continue their favorite activities. Being told that they will be allowed to do so is a great relief to them.

161

Parents who belong to a religious community should inform the minister or rabbi of the shared parenting plan so that he or she doesn't put your child on the spot by saying "We missed you last week." Sunday school teachers should also be informed. Both can reassure your child that she continues to be a part of the community regardless of her parents' divorce. To leave the community entirely would uproot children from their friends and from the comfort their religion can bring.

Mark has friends at school who live near us and two older friends on David's street. Because of our time-sharing arrangement, we quickly realized that none of his school chums would ever see his other home and meet his dad unless David arranged for them to visit on the weekend. Mark was very pleased to be able to bring his friends to his other home if for no other reason than to prove that he did have a fish tank! A little extra driving, a larger allowance to cover bus fare, or more telephone time is a small price to pay to keep your school-age child's friendships intact.

Your Adolescent

8

Being a parent takes time, good-quality time. I think kids should be considered an asset rather than a liability. And you should let them know they're an asset.

During the turbulent adolescent years, a young person develops his own self-image. A positive self-image enables a child to deal with the changes of adolescence — his new body image, sexual awareness and intellectual growth. Whether his view of himself is positive or negative depends largely on his parents' love, support and active involvement in his life. For this reason, some researchers believe that a breakdown in parenting after separation or divorce may be more significant for teenagers than the ending of the marriage itself. Adolescents are at risk when they are deprived of relationships with their fathers. As researcher Judith Wallerstein points out in *Second Chances*, "Without the continued support of their fathers . . . boys lack self-confidence and pride in their own masculinity. The issue, although different, is just as serious for girls. Afflicted with a sense of longing and rejection, they too feel hurt, unsure of their femininity, and insecure in their relationships with men."

Other areas of a young person's life may also be affected by separation and divorce. These include his relationship with his peer group, coaches, neighbors and other adults, and his ability to continue with ongoing activities outside his family. Although these may seem replaceable to his parents — "He's young. He'll make new friends" — they are extremely important to him and the developmental stage he is at. If you ever had to move from one high school to another as a teenager, you will probably remember the emotional upheaval it caused and the time it took to recover. All these factors, therefore, should be considered when you and your coparent are discussing the separation and its possible effects on your teenager.

BREAKING THE NEWS

The same guidelines you would follow in telling a school-age child about the ending of your marriage apply to an adolescent. If possible, tell him together, provide honest but not overly detailed reasons for the separation and emphasize that he is not to blame. Most teenagers will have a fairly good idea of what the problems in the marriage have been, but this doesn't relieve parents of the responsibility of giving reasons and discussing the consequences of the separation with their elder children.

Reactions during the mourning process after separation will vary from child to child. Some adolescents will seem very tired, have difficulty concentrating or cry frequently. Others may hide their feelings of anger and sadness and withdraw into a shell. A child may be judgmental and side with the parent he feels has been wronged or, if the level of tension and conflict has been high between the parents, he may say he is washing his hands of both of them. In an attempt to escape the turmoil of his family situation, he may spend considerably more time with friends.

This is a time to open up the lines of communication with your teen, at the same time avoiding the temptation to treat him as a confidante. Parents who consider their adolescent their best friend are meeting their emotional needs through their child instead of through relationships with other adults. They often send mixed messages to their teens — telling them to go out and have a good time but letting them know that they will be lonely without them. As counselors point out, the danger in this type of role reversal is that the nurturing process is turned upside down. Young adults who have been parent nurturers find it difficult to leave home and make a life for themselves. Guilt-ridden, they may live according to their parent's wishes and needs rather than their own. Intimate relationships with others may be difficult due to fear of commitment or an inability to receive love.

During the adjustment period after separation, an adolescent may be ashamed or embarrassed by the changes in his family. It is important to emphasize that you are still a family and that both parents will continue to love and care for him. Being available to your child at this difficult time is one way to prove your commitment to him. Teens still need their parents and, although they wouldn't admit it, don't like to be left for long stretches of time on their own. Isolina Ricci in *Mom's House, Dad's House* recommends setting up anchors for teens who are left on their own after school — "a mainstay adult close by who knows what to do and whom to call in an emergency; a series of check-in phone calls between parent and child through the week; a routine that both can count on; and a good set of house and safety rules." Don't be surprised, though, if even when you do make yourself available, your teen confides in someone outside the family rather than you; it is normal for this age group to talk about their feelings with people to whom they are less emotionally attached.

Counselors also suggest writing letters to your adolescent expressing your love and hopes for the future. A note before your first separation from your child might be helpful. This is a time when your teen needs reassurance, and having your letter to read during sad times may help if he is uncomfortable talking on the phone to you.

A TEEN'S CONCERNS

Their mother and I frequently find that the kids' activities take precedence over ours. Going to a party is not essential to middle-aged people, but to teenagers, it's crucial that they make every one. You realize that's how they feel and you try to accommodate them as much as possible.

Shared parenting of an adolescent differs from shared parenting of a younger child in several significant ways. What appeals to a six- to ten-year-old about a coparenting arrangement—two birthdays, two holidays, two pets—is insignificant to a teenager. Having two birthday parties with your family isn't such a hot thing. What matters most to him is his life outside the family and the impact the separation will have on it.

Although they should be told that their parents will make the final decision, children who are older than thirteen can be consulted about the choice of parenting plan. If they are not consulted, they will likely accuse their parents of treating them "like babies." In general, year-by-year or day-to-day plans do not suit a teenager's lifestyle. Many adolescents prefer to stay in one home with the flexibility to see the other parent for overnights, meals and other activities. In this plan, some type of routine is usually set up with the out-of-house parent; for example, a certain night is always reserved for dinner. Other teens prefer to spend the school year with one parent and vacations with the other parent in addition to frequent visits. A separation agreement with a parenting plan involving adolescents works best if it has built-in flexibility or recognition that the plan may be changed as the years go by. Parents thus still share the decision making, but the time-sharing may vary according to the needs of the child and the parents.

Like elementary schoolchildren, adolescents need to be assured that they will still be able to participate in extracurricular activities. Parents who help to ensure that their adolescent's activities continue are assisting their child in two ways: they are providing him with continuity and the support of friends at a difficult time, as well as a release from the emotional stress of separation. Sports, in particular, are helpful in this way. Parents can also help by checking that a good balance is struck between chores, schoolwork and their child's social life. Although the development of a sense of responsibility is a strength that adolescents in single-parent families acquire, too much responsibility can have an adverse effect on a teen's social life and, subsequently, on his self-esteem. A child who is forced to take the place of the absent parent, or who must spend a great deal of his time caring for younger siblings, may not be able to enjoy the social life with his peers that is an important part of this developmental stage.

Part-time jobs may play an important part in this balancing act. As the fast-food industry and the number of stores with longer hours have grown, the number of students working part-time has increased dramatically.

The added money and personal sense of achievement gained by your child from a part-time job are obvious pluses; however, there are several things to keep in mind before agreeing to your child's working. Some educators warn that teenagers who work more than fifteen hours a week are risking failure at school. Canadian high-school students surveyed for a study on dropouts said that, when they worked more than twenty-one hours a week, their homework and marks suffered. They also felt that it made them tired and irritable. The time and energy diverted from schoolwork to working is also diverted from extra-curricular activities, which means that both outside interests and social life are restricted. Some parents agree to their child's working on the condition that he will quit the job if his marks suffer.

PROBLEMS LATER ON

Our lives revolved around Barry and his moods. Living with him was like being with a two-year-old who just won't stop screaming. We wondered how we were going to survive. It was that kind of pressure and tension. We tiptoed around so he wouldn't get mad.

At a time when you, yourself, may be experiencing various mid-life crises, coupled with a marital separation, it may seem impossible to deal with the mood swings of insecure adolescents. When adolescent acting out does occur, counselors recommend that parents should try to overlook the minor rule-breaking and deal with the major outbursts as calmly as possible. Responding with angry words to angry words from your teen just escalates an argument. Positive behavior, on the other hand, should be met with affectionate approval.

Parents who treat their children in a democratic, rather than autocratic, way by making decisions that affect them *with* them may be better able to guide their children through problems that occur in the teen years. Using what some counselors call "I messages" rather than "you messages" helps build a positive relationship with adolescents. An "I message" expresses a problem in terms of your own concerns or feelings and is nonjudgmental — "I don't think it's fair that I have had to tidy up after you in the bathroom every morning this week. What can we do to solve the problem?" A "you message" is accusatory and results in arguments rather than discussions — "You're nothing but a little slob. It's impossible living with you." Teenagers don't need parents who agree with everything they say, but they do need parents who will talk with them, not *at* them, and who will listen to their point of view, without demeaning them for having different opinions.

Although adolescents need autonomy, they also need security and guidance from parents — a firm base from which they can fly and return. In a flexible shared parenting arrangement, it is important that a teenager not be allowed to slip between the two homes. Children have been known to tell one parent that they are going to visit the other, only to go off with friends. Parents must still set limits and check with the other parent when a change in plans is made.

AGE-APPROPRIATE BEHAVIOR OF TEENAGERS
As with elementary schoolchildren, when problems do occur, it is important to be familiar with behavior patterns that may occur at various developmental stages during adolescence rather than blaming each problem on the divorce. Not all teens will follow these patterns precisely,

but they will give you an idea of what to expect in the years to come.

Thirteen
- Inner-directed and often moody as he struggles with physical and emotional changes of adolescence
- Standoffish; rejects questions by parents as prying
- Sensitive to real or imagined criticism
- Worries about everything—appearance, school, future
- Frequently annoyed by younger brothers and sisters

Fourteen
- More outgoing and less guarded than at thirteen because he has learned to cope with changes
- Expresses feelings more openly
- Relationships within family usually less tense

Fifteen
- Period of disequilibrium; may be guarded and uncommunicative as he struggles with self-identity and knowledge that childhood is ending
- Begins in earnest to separate himself from parents
- Rebels against authority at home and school
- Prefers peers or own company to family; may refuse to go on family outings

Sixteen
- More even disposition; more self-assured and outgoing
- Still prefers to spend time outside home rather than with family

Studies have shown that adverse effects of divorce on adolescents are most pronounced when there is a combination of multiple changes in their lives and ongoing parental conflict. Hostility between parents may produce anxiety, lower self-esteem and a loss of self-control. If the focus of the conflict between a mother and father shifts after the end of the marriage from personal habits of a spouse to issues affecting their child, the discord may have even greater adverse effects on teenagers. Adolescent adjustment problems can include depression, drug use, violence, promiscuous sexual behavior, truancy and drastic changes in their choice of friends.

Parents may find it difficult to differentiate between true depression and the normal moodiness of adolescence. Warning signs of depression include intense feelings of worthlessness and hopelessness about the future, loss of interest in previously enjoyed activities, frequent crying, sudden rage, problems in concentration, withdrawing from friends, or appetite and sleep changes. Counselors advise that, if these changes persist beyond a few weeks, professional help should be sought.

Although many teenagers experiment with drugs, those who lack a strong self-identity and who have not been allowed to express angry feelings verbally may abuse drugs to strike back at their parents. If your child suddenly starts behaving in an uncharacteristic, erratic fashion and you suspect he may be involved in drugs, confronting him in an angry way may lead to denial and further alienation. Your public health department or a drug rehabilitation center can provide you with information about drugs and how to help your child overcome the problem.

An adolescent's violence toward family members and those outside the family is the most obvious expression of anger. When children have not been taught to express their anger in healthy ways, they may lash out physically. Parent abuse, in particular, is profoundly disturbing for parents. Help may not be sought because of the shame and isolation that is felt by the abused parent. In this situation, it may be helpful to know that abuse of mothers and fathers by their sons and daughters happens in all kinds of families thousands of times a year across Canada. Socioeconomic status, a divorce or the type of custody arrangement have no bearing on parent abuse. If you are being abused, help is available for both you and your child.

Violence between adolescents and parents isn't talked about very often. It doesn't get talked about because of the immense shame everybody feels. I know of people to whom it's happening and none of them are asking for help, because it's just too painful.

In the case of sexual behavior, studies seem to indicate that adolescents whose parents have divorced begin having intercourse earlier than their peers. Some researchers believe that this may be due to a lack of parenting after divorce. Being available to your child, discussing the emotional aspects of sexual activity and setting reasonable rules governing a teenager's social life are as important after divorce as they were before.

Seeking help for the minor and major problems that may occur after a marital separation is an act of love. Depending on your community, many options are open to you and your teenager. At an age when peer acceptance is important, group meetings of teens whose parents have separated or divorced can be invaluable for some children. Ask at your child's high school if a group has been set up or how you could become involved in forming one (see page 159), or contact your family service association. Support groups for parents experiencing crises in dealing with a teen have also been set up in some communities. Individual counseling or family therapy through which the family is treated as a unit are also available (see page 93).

Changing the Time-Sharing Arrangement

At one point I asked my fourteen-year-old, "How do you like this business of going back and forth?" and she said, "Just fine. You're not thinking of changing it are you?" And I said, "No, I was just asking the question." And she said, "Well, it's just fine, Mother. About the time I can't stand you for one second longer, it's time to go back to Dad."

As children grow older, they may resent what they see as the intrusion of a shared parenting plan on their lives. Some may request longer periods of time at each home or may want to choose one home as their primary residence. Others will be content to continue the time-sharing plan they have always had. Still others feel stuck in the plan their parents have set up for them.

Adolescents in the last group may be afraid of hurting the feelings of the parent whose home is not chosen as a base. Those with younger sisters and brothers provide consistent support for their siblings as they travel back and forth between homes. They may worry about the effect of "abandoning" their siblings, at the same time resenting the responsibility. Sometimes they will experiment with a change in the schedule by finding an excuse to remain at one home while the other children go to the other home. They'll test the waters to see if the younger group will be all right without them. In these situations there can be a high level of frustration, a feeling of wanting to change the plan, but not knowing how to go about it.

The introduction of a stepparent can also influence where an adolescent wants to live. When Catherine and Alex were fourteen and twelve, their father remarried. Their new stepmother had never had children of her own and found it difficult adapting to living with two children for two-week periods. She took a particular dislike to Alex. The father and stepmother came to the conclusion that, because she wasn't especially well suited to a mothering role, he would take over all of the responsibility for the children and she would have nothing to do with them. Catherine and Alex responded by spending most of their time in their rooms, keeping out of the way. Catherine describes this period as "not living at Dad's, but hiding out there." When it became obvious that this was not working for anyone in the family, a change was made to the parenting plan. The children are currently trying out three weeks with their mother and one week and two weekends with their father and stepmother.

Parents can help adolescents who may be in time-sharing quandaries by saying from time to time that the schedule isn't written in stone and that they are open to discussing changes to it.

As you parent your adolescent after divorce, it might be helpful to know that the 1984 Project Teen Canada study conducted by Reginald Bibby and Donald Posterski found that ". . . as a whole, teenagers from homes of divorced, separated, and widowed parents differ little from other teenagers. Considering the conflict and pain commonly associated with divorce and death, the ability of young people to adjust to their altered circumstances is often remarkable. Once removed from the limbo of separation, children of divorced parents, along with the widowed, hold attitudes about the future that are not dampened by their situations at home. Their feelings about getting married, having children, and family life generally remain undaunted."

The New Extended Family

9

One great thing about joint custody is that you can have a relationship with another person and not bring him into your child's life until you're ready to make a commitment. It was scary the first time the man who would become my second husband was at my home for breakfast with my son. Here I was making a commitment again. Because he didn't have children of his own, I thought he was incredibly wonderful to take both of us into his life.

O n Valentine's Day, my son receives cards from his mother, father, stepfather, two sets of grandparents, my stepgrandmother, his stepgrandmother, aunts and uncles, a stepuncle and a stepsister. As we look through these cards, I marvel at the number of important people in Mark's life and the variety of experiences and support they have provided. He is growing up in an extended family, albeit a different type of extended family from the norm, with its own set of special strengths and problems.

YOUR PARENTS

My parents were furious at me. They thought I had been a lousy wife who hadn't been able to keep the marriage together, which angered me no end. It made me say things that I regretted afterward.

On the day I was married, my mother told me that she could die happily because now I had someone to take care of me. On the day I ended the marriage, she began taking sleeping pills.

Telling your parents about your decision to end your marriage can be almost as difficult as telling your child. They may feel as if your divorce is their divorce. Your loss, their loss. One woman's mother accused her bitterly of "destroying my little family." A man's father, who adored his daughter-in-law, berated his son endlessly about his failures as a husband. Parents who stayed together "for the sake of the children" may question the values of those who would not do the same, especially when there has been no physical abuse and their child's marriage has always appeared to be better than their own. They worry about you. They worry about their grandchildren. And they worry about themselves.

We cannot have high expectations of our parents at this time. This is a stage in their lives when parents may need and expect support from their adult children. When your marriage ends, you may revert to a dependent status in your parents' minds, if not in the physical sense. Borrowing money and extra baby-sitting are insignificant worries compared with the deep concerns they may have about you and your children. Initially, there is a high level of shock, frustration, disappointment, anger and worry. Like all family members, parents need time to adjust, and you have to accept the fact that, depending on their personalities and the family history, your mother or father or both may never completely accept your new life.

The concept of shared parenting may seem very

foreign to them. A mother may be appalled that her daughter is willingly sharing childcare duties with her former husband: "But a child needs his mother to tuck him in every night." A father may be puzzled at his son's enthusiasm for parenting at the expense of his career: "But you've worked so hard to get where you are. Are you sure you want to do this?" Sharing your reasons for deciding upon shared parenting with your parents and emphasizing the commitment you and your former partner feel are first steps in enlisting their support. Your parents may need to observe life in a shared parenting family and see its benefits before they are convinced. In the meantime, you can help shield your children from their skepticism by setting up some groundrules. Grandparents should be asked to refrain from making negative comments about the parenting plan, from criticizing the other parent in front of the child, from making the child feel stuck in the middle, and from probing for information about the other parent.

Grandparents who take these guidelines to heart can be invaluable to their grandchildren. Various researchers have found that children benefit from a close relationship with at least one grandparent. This is particularly true of children whose parents are divorced. After David and I separated, Mark continued to spend every Thursday afternoon at my mother's. His Grams would give him her undivided love for an afternoon, in the same way she always had. During the adjustment period, a grandparent's home is a refuge, a place to get away for awhile from too many confusing, changing things.

Studies have shown that, when a daughter divorces, the grandchildren's contact with their grandparents is usually maintained or in some cases becomes more frequent. The opposite is true of sons. Although it has been said that this is probably because most fathers do not have custody of their children, another reason may be that women tend to take the initiative when it comes to visiting parents. One man whose children were preschoolers when he began shared parenting with their mother remembers being thankful that he did involve his parents in his life at that time. When he visited them, it gave him a respite from parenting, the grandparents enjoyed playing with the children, and the children benefited from the attention they received.

Your coparent's relationship with your parents can be a sensitive issue. The best scenario is when grandparents provide support to their child, but keep the door open to the former spouse. It is important to remember that your parents didn't divorce this person, you did. If they've formed a close relationship with your former partner, it is unrealistic to expect them to sever their ties because you have severed yours. It is also unrealistic to expect them immediately to change their ways of interacting with you and your former mate on issues affecting your child. One example of this is the father who consults his former son-in-law rather than his daughter about financial matters concerning his grandson. Another is the mother who phones her former daughter-in-law rather than her son to ask about knitting a sweater for her granddaughter. Gentle reminders of your own competence in these matters may help your parents to make the adjustment.

My daughter's father has maintained friendships with my family. He's always liked my folks and my sister, so he goes over there with Marla. It bothered me at first, but my mother just said, "Well, we like him and Marla's our granddaughter and it gives us a chance to see more of her." I finally realized that it was good for Marla to see all this normal stuff going on. I guess at first I thought they should choose sides, but now it doesn't bother me.

Some coparents find it difficult to continue a relationship with their former in-laws. In the adjustment period, if a father- and mother-in-law feel that their child has been wronged, they may react with coldness or anger when contacted. Others may feel ill at ease. Former sons- or daughters-in-law may blame their former in-laws for their coparent's shortcomings. In some families, it may simply be a case of letting the healing process take its course after the divorce and trying again when the family has recovered. In other families, the contact is broken forever to the detriment of the children involved.

DATING AND REPARTNERING

I have had one relationship, a woman with two children who were the same ages as my children. To me the fit wasn't right, so I didn't want to go any further. It was my eldest who especially resented the times that we all spent together. My ex-wife, on the other hand, was involved early on with a man who doesn't have any children and that seemed to make it easier. They've been living together for three years now.

My philosophy about dating was to let the children cope with one thing at a time. They never saw me with anyone else for two or three years. I was comfortable with that for awhile and then it changed when I became seriously involved. I did things according to what felt right.

Unlike sole custody parents, parents who coparent have more time to enjoy a social life on the days that they don't have their children living with them. Dating on "off-days" will avoid compounding a child's fears of abandonment directly after the separation. A child exposed to his parent's dating at this time may see his parent's new friend as a rival for his love and attention and may be deeply distressed. Some parents find socializing with their children at single parents' events, church activities or neighborhood functions a way to ease back into a social life without upsetting their sons or daughters.

Later, when your children are more settled and confident, may be a better time to talk to them about the fact that you will be dating, that, like them, parents need friends too, and that your going out with other adults has nothing to do with not wanting to be with them. Counselors generally agree that it is preferable not to introduce your children to a casual date, because it can cause confusion and anxiety for them. Wait until you are as certain as you can be that the relationship will be an ongoing one.

Stepping into a new relationship can be wonderful and intimidating at the same time, doubly so when one person has children, triply so when the other one does too. Taking the time to consider everyone's feelings and needs, and making changes slowly, is the advice that many coparents give. The new person in your life and your children need time to get to know one another. Your love is not a magic thread that can tie all of you together happily ever after. A new companion and your children need time with you and time without you to develop their own relationship free of high expectations and demands on your part.

For many coparents, achieving a balance between their commitment to their children and their commitment to a new partner is challenging. For example, when a man's home changes from being a place where he is nurtured to being a place where he nurtures, there may be a definite shift in his priorities. His children often become the first priority in his life. A new partner may accept playing second fiddle to his children in the short term, but is unlikely to want to accept a long-term engagement. Although most coparents describe themselves as "package deals," it is unfair to expect a new partner not to want to come first at least part of the time.

If you are considering remarriage or cohabitation, "who comes first when" is only one of many questions to discuss with your significant other before making a final decision. Other questions to consider carefully include:

- What are your reasons for considering remarriage or cohabitation?
- Have your children been given enough time to grieve the ending of their parents' marriage?
- Have they been given plenty of opportunity to get to know your new partner well?
- What are your child-rearing philosophies? Are they compatible?
- Where will you live and what repercussions will that have on the children and the time-sharing arrangement(s) that you have?
- Is your new partner aware of the limitations your separation agreement places on moving to another area. Will this cause any problems in the future?
- Will your new partner be able to handle the regular contact with your coparent that shared parenting involves?
- How will you handle your finances?
- Who will do what chores?
- What will children call family members?
- Do you want children of your own?

If both people have children:

- Have the children been given the opportunity to get to know one another well?
- What chores have each parent's children been doing; will they change?
- Will children have to share rooms?
- If both parents have been coparenting, will the schedules mesh? How will they need to be changed?

The decision to remarry or cohabit obviously affects shared parenting arrangements in significant ways. As stepfamily experts Emily and John Visher warn in *Stepfamilies*, the addition of another parental figure "can at times throw a previously relaxed custody arrangement into disarray." Issues that may have been settled long ago—financial arrangements, location of the children's second home, time-sharing plans—can be placed in question when a stepparent joins the family. The old hurtful feelings aroused by these issues are also likely to return.

It is the re-emergence of mistrust that can be most damaging to the parenting partnership. Like the children, the coparent needs reassurance that the new partner has no intention of replacing him in his role. Faced with this prospect, some coparents have panicked and gone to court to sue for sole custody. As one mother recalls of this period, "My coparent had crazy ideas about my new partner. He thought that he was a monster. Even though his sane self knew that he wasn't, his hurt self was saying, 'This monster is going to damage my children.' "

This is a time for the coparent who is considering remarriage to reaffirm his or her commitment to shared parenting with the other parent. For the other parent it may be helpful to know that his or her negative feelings and fears surrounding the coparent's remarriage are common. "Don't let the flashback emotions get the upper hand," suggests counselor Isolina Ricci in *Mom's House, Dad's House.* "Stick to your business relationship instead." As for the stepparent, his or her neutrality, patience and sensitivity to the former partner's fears can help everyone during this time of change.

Forming a stepfamily is an enormous step that requires much soul-searching and discussion before it is taken. You might want to consider remarriage counseling with a counselor or therapist who is familiar with the problems of stepfamilies. There are many good books on the subject (see Selected Bibliography). If your shared parenting plan needs to be renegotiated, follow the steps you followed in setting it up originally, and remember that outside help is available.

STEPPARENTING

Helen has done a brilliant job of stepmothering. She gave Trevor the space to be unfriendly toward her at first and let him come to her in his own time. She's made it absolutely clear that she's not his mother; I am. She's his stepmother and that's a different relationship. One of the issues that was such a concern for me was that an ex-husband's partner will be an enormous influence on a child's life. You have no control over who their stepmother will be. Some of Barry's early girlfriends looked awfully ditzy to me. Helen was such a relief. You don't really share parenting with your ex-husband alone. You share it with your ex-husband's wife too.

Coparents who merge two families or add a stepparent often place unrealistic expectations on stepparents and children. They may expect stepparents to love their children and their children to love and obey their stepparents. However, love takes time and nourishment, and even "liking" is not always easy to accomplish on a regular basis. In the beginning, a stepfamily is an emotional brew stirred by many seen and unseen hands.

Eight years ago Tom and Elaine began living together. Tom had two boys from his first marriage, Paul and Simon, who were both preschoolers. At that time his shared parenting arrangement with his former wife involved an every-other-day time-sharing plan. Both remember those early years as tense. Elaine found it difficult to adjust to a life that changed on a daily basis. The boys didn't take to her nor she to them. She found herself resenting the undivided attention they received from Tom and the role that she felt she was increasingly being forced to take on — that of limit-setter. Neither had discussed a child-rearing philosophy ahead of time; consequently, Elaine's need to set some limits clashed with Tom's need to be a nurturer and giver.

The tension caused by Elaine's confusion about what she could insist on in terms of the children's behavior and Tom's lack of support in this area took a turn for the worse when the children left for their other home. Elaine would feel enormously relieved, which irritated Tom, who missed his children. Neither had any compassion for the other's perspective. Looking back, Tom admits that "the first thing for me to learn was that limits were necessary for Elaine to feel comfortable in our home and, for them to work, I had to be committed to them. It wasn't enough for me to say to her, 'Go ahead and set limits.' For the limits to be accepted, the boys had to know that I was behind them."

It has only been recently that Tom and Elaine have

felt that their family was a "real family, a foursome." Part of their success they attribute to counseling. Part to the age of the children. And part to two new members of the family—both dogs. "The dogs belong to all of us. When the kids are here, I can play with them while Tom is being a dad. Then I don't feel so isolated. They've been an amazing help to me."

Stepmothers and fathers without children themselves step bravely into the foreign territory of family life generally unprepared for the problems that await them. Problems can come from many different directions—a new in-law who calls you by her former daughter-in-law's name, a former spouse who refuses to attend a school function if you are going to be there, a child who says, "I love this place so much. It's too bad you live here." The best you can do is to ease into the situation gradually. Try the friend, rather than parent, approach with the kids. Don't come on too strong, but don't be remote either— just be yourself. If you're tempted to complain about the children or the difficulties of your new life, rant and rave to someone outside the home and return with clear, unemotional information to discuss with your new family.

There are several family combinations possible when the new couple both have children. In my own family, my partner Erich has a six-year-old daughter who lives with us every other weekend and on holidays. Because Alyssa's primary residence with her mother is in another community, he takes her out for supper midweek after work rather than seeing her at our home. Our situation is a little bit different than most shared parenting and sole custody combined families because Mark is not at our home for fourteen evenings each month. The time he spends with Erich is thus not appreciably longer than the time Alyssa spends with her father. Parents in this type of stepfamily are usually painfully aware of the jealousies that can be aroused when a parent does spend more time with a stepchild than with his or her own child. In our family, Wednesday evenings are Alyssa's evenings with her dad and Thursday evenings are Mark's with Erich. Our weekends are coordinated so we are all together at the same time.

Like other stepfamilies, our life is spent fine-tuning. Although our children already knew and liked each other, we began stepparenting with two preschoolers in the middle of their heavy-duty Oedipal phase. If Erich so much as put his arm around me, Alyssa was between us in a flash, very good-humoredly, but there nonetheless. Mark invented a game called "The Big Bad Fox," a rather complicated version of tag, which enabled him to vent his emotions against Erich all in the guise of a game. Mark's relationship with Erich improved dramatically after they started building models together on Thursday nights. It was a special activity that gave their relationship a focus. Alyssa and I have always had an easygoing friendship; however, after our first weekend together, Alyssa let us know that she wanted to spend more time with her father alone, a perfectly reasonable request. In stepfamilies, the need of children to spend time alone with their own parent is sometimes ignored in the rush to do "family-type things."

We were very aware of the problems that might occur in beginning stepparenting in what had been Mark's and my home. We didn't want Alyssa to feel like an intruder any more than we wanted Mark to feel displaced. To help Alyssa feel at home, we used all her familiar sheets and comforters from her father's apartment, tacked up her pictures on the bedroom wall, set photographs of her on tables, a special new towel on the towel rack and her toothbrush in the stand in the bathroom. My materialistic son was receptive to having most of Alyssa's toys available to be played with throughout the week (in the beginning we put away her "special" toys), and he also looked forward to having a playmate every other weekend. Both kids were excited by the prospect of having their own playroom in the basement. Up until that point the basement had been used for storage. Although we simply painted the concrete walls white and plunked down a carpet remnant, it was the first joint venture planned by our new family, and for the children represented something that was "theirs" rather than "mine" or "yours."

Our next step was helping Alyssa ease into the more relaxed atmosphere of our home compared with her other home. Along with her toys and stuffed animals, every weekend she used to bring a verbal list of rules and regulations — "Mommy says I have to do this. Mommy says I have to do that." Like Mark, she now knows that different homes have different rules.

We all miss Alyssa when she isn't with us. Sunday nights, when just one child is tucked into bed upstairs, can be subdued. Overall, though, we have been incredibly lucky in the "fit" of our two families. Much luckier than some.

A few years after Diana had separated, she met Alan. His marriage had recently ended and he was in the process of setting up a shared parenting arrangement for his three-year-old daughter. The following year, Alan and Tanya moved into the house that Diana shared with her seven-year-old daughter, Mary, and her five-year-old son, Daniel. Diana also had a shared parenting plan; however, whereas her plan was one week on, one week off, Alan's was Tuesdays, Thursdays and alternate weekends. As Diana remembers, "We needed a schedule on the front door. We could never remember who was going to be where when."

Mary disliked Alan and extended her lack of affection to his daughter. "It was just too hard," says Diana. After a year and a half, Alan moved into another house nearby. Nine years later, Diana and he have a relationship that has continued off and on over the years. "So much of it gets easier as the kids get older. They're much less dependent. You don't have as much influence, and what you do doesn't have as much effect. At this point Mary thinks Alan is OK, but it just doesn't matter anymore. It doesn't matter to Mary if she likes him or doesn't like him."

Unlike Diana and Alan, some coparents have found it an advantage to stepparent with another person who has a shared parenting arrangement. Both new partners hold similar beliefs in the benefits of coparenting, understand the extra effort it takes and accept the required contact with the former partner.

In the end, though, it is not the type of family combination or the fit of the various family members that determines the emotional health of a stepfamily, but the relationship of the couple itself. As Erna Paris in her book *Stepfamilies: Making Them Work* writes: "The second-marriage couple who married principally because they wanted to (and not to provide a substitute parent, housekeeper/babysitter, or meal ticket) will more likely survive the almost inevitable disruption that such family reorganization brings in its wake. The couple creates the framework. It is they who root the tree in the earth, and from that base, other relationships become less difficult. The strong couple at the center will give a clear message to upset, angry children that they have every intention of making this marriage work. They will also be less vulnerable to the disruptions of ex-spouses and more able (and willing) to cooperate for the children's sake."

YOUR CHILD HAS A STEPPARENT AND STEPSIBLINGS

His father is not athletic in the least and doesn't have the patience to deal with our son's temper tantrums or defeatist attitude when he's trying to learn something new. His step-dad is the exact opposite. He likes sports and is the soul of patience. Now that Nathan is more interested in sports, he relies on his step-dad to help him out. His dad attends the games, but it's his step-dad who is his practice buddy.

More than one-third of North American children live in families in which one, if not both, parents are remarried. There is a distinct possibility, then, that your child may have a stepparent and possibly stepsiblings at some point in his life. It has been suggested that children in coparenting arrangements adapt better to life in a stepfamily than do children in sole custody arrangements; however, factors other than the parenting plan come into play as well.

Age is one. The younger the child is, the easier it will be for her to adapt. Preschoolers who have been given the time to mourn after their parents' divorce and whose parents have developed a parenting relationship free of turmoil are often able to accept a caring stepparent into their lives fairly quickly. Adolescents, on the other hand, tend to have a more difficult time. They are asked to participate in the formation of a new family during a period when they are trying to separate from the family. A loss of status in the family may also cause problems. As one father recalls, "There was some friction between my second wife and my eldest daughter. It was like two people trying to run the same place." School-age children fall somewhere between the two extremes. They often become rivals for the attention of their opposite-sex parent, feel concerned about being seen as different by their friends and suffer from feelings of divided loyalty.

The issue of divided loyalty can be minimized if the coparents have a good parenting relationship and stress that the stepparent is not a replacement for one of the parents. A comparison can be made between stepparents and baby-sitters, who are different from parents but who take care of children in the same way as mothers and fathers do. In addition, a coparent who is positive about the relationship between his or her child and the stepparent in the other home gives a youngster permission to develop the relationship free of concerns about how it might affect that parent.

If your child has a new stepparent, be prepared for negative behavior changes as he copes with these new changes in his family. It will take time for him to accept another adult into his life. Counselors suggest that parents wait a few months and, if the acting out continues, consider getting some professional help for their child. After a child adjusts to life in a stepfamily, a stepparent can benefit him by providing another role model and diverse experiences from which to learn and grow.

Stepparents and stepchildren generally have a more difficult time adjusting to one another than stepsiblings. Emily and John Visher (*Stepfamilies: Myths and Realities*) believe that the reason for this may be that the expectations for a sibling relationship are lower. Because parents expect siblings to fight, stepsiblings seldom feel forced to care for one another. The relationship is allowed to develop without the pressure of expectation of "instant love." Be that as it may, some stepsiblings do have difficulty. An eldest child who is no longer the eldest may need special help in adjusting. Opposite-sex adolescents may also find living together stressful. A new baby in the family can be a positive or negative addition for siblings. If only one of the spouses has children, and the children don't get along well with the stepparent or haven't been given time to adjust to stepfamily life, a new child may be resented and feared as a rival for the parent's love.

On the other hand, a new baby in the family can bring stepsiblings closer together or provide some much-needed personal space for an only child.

I think Patrick was relieved when each set of parents had a new baby. Although occasionally he regrets no longer being the sole focus, having younger brothers certainly takes some of the pressure off. In the beginning, he had four parents whose complete focus was on him and that's pretty intense for any kid. He couldn't sneeze that phone calls didn't start. Now, of course, we're so busy working and raising our other kids too, that Patrick gets to be just one of the group.

Afterword

A s you load a bicycle into a car trunk for the ump-teenth time, or as you lie awake in bed missing your children, or as you struggle to maintain your composure during a disagreement with your coparent, you may have doubts about the parenting plan you have chosen. In fact, you may not just have doubts about it — you may actively curse it.

Shared parenting is not a magic potion for divorced families. It takes time for the wounds of divorce to heal and for the rhythm of life as a shared parenting family to be accepted by every member of the family. It also takes hard work, negotiation, commitment and more. There are going to be days when you're not capable of being the perfect coparent, just as there were days before the separation when you weren't the perfect mother or father.

On the days when nothing seems to be going right, I try to reflect on why Mark's father and I chose shared parenting. I remember that our commitment to being full-time parents to our child didn't stop when our marriage ended. I remember that our son has been able to continue meaningful relationships with both of us while living in two homes. I take pride in our being able to work things out regarding Mark, as difficult as that sometimes can be.

I think of the wonderful times we each have watching and helping our son grow and learn from day to day, not just on a limited weekend basis. And, finally, I try to imagine what it would be like to have the emotional and financial weight of child-rearing resting on my shoulders alone. When I remember all of these things, I feel incredibly lucky.

Given the right circumstances and personalities, shared parenting is a viable and increasingly popular parenting plan after a marriage ends. It is working for children who are able to adapt to living in two homes, who feel loved and cared for by their parents, and who are free of the stress of constant parental conflict. And it is working for parents who are able to cooperate in giving their children the gift of time with both of them.

Resource List

FAMILY COUNSELING AND DIVORCE MEDIATION
SERVICES

Canada

Family Mediation Canada
123 Woolwich St.
Guelph, Ontario
N1M 3V1
(519) 836-7750

Contact for listings for private mediators across the country.

Newfoundland

Unified Family Court
21 King's Bridge Rd.
St. John's, Nfld.
A1C 3K4
(709) 753-5873

Prince Edward Island

Unified Family Court
Department of Justice
42 Water St.
P.O. Box 2900
Charlottetown, P.E.I.
C1A 8C1
(902) 892-9131

Nova Scotia

Atlantic Child Guidance Centre
1464 Tower Rd.
Halifax, N.S.
B3H 4L4
(902) 422-1611

Family Service Association of Halifax, Dartmouth,
Bedford and Halifax County
5614 Fenwick St.
Ste. 106
Halifax, N.S.
B3H 1P9
(902) 420-1980

New Brunswick

Court of Queen's Bench of New Brunswick
Family Division
Justice Bldg.
Queen St.
Room 207
Fredericton, N.B.
E3B 5H1
(506) 453-2015

Court of Queen's Bench of New Brunswick
Family Division
770 Main St.
Moncton, N.B.
E1C 8R3
(506) 858-2710

Court of Queen's Bench
Family Division
P.O. Box 6398
Stn. "A"
Saint John, N.B.
E2L 4J4
(506) 658-2560

Quebec

Service de la médiation à la famille
Chambre de la Famille
Cour supérieure
1, rue Notre-Dame E.
Montreal, P.Q.
H2Y 1B6
(514) 873-5868

Service de médiation
300, boulevard Jean-Lesage
Bureau 254
Quebec City, P.Q.
G1K 8L2
(418) 643-8315

Ontario

Unified Family Court
55 Main St. W.
Hamilton, Ont.
L8P 1H4
(416) 525-1550

Frontenac Family Referral Service
469 Montreal St.
Kingston, Ont.
K7L 4X8
(613) 548-6795

Family Service London
90 Albert St.
London, Ont.
N6A 1L8
(519) 433-0183

Families in Transition
Family Service Association of Metro Toronto
14 College St.
Toronto, Ont.
M5P 2V8
(416) 922-3144

Family Court Toronto
311 Jarvis St.
Toronto, Ont.
M5B 2E4
(416) 923-7781

Jewish Family and Child Service
4600 Bathurst St.
Willowdale, Ont.
M2R 3V3
(416) 638-7800

Manitoba

Family Conciliation
405 Broadway
9th Flr.
Winnipeg, Man.
R3N 0H6
(204) 945-7236

Saskatchewan

Unified Family Court
224 4th Ave. S.
Saskatoon, Sask.
S7K 2H6
(306) 933-5174

Alberta

Calgary Family Service Bureau
120 13th Ave. SE
Calgary, Alberta
T2G 1B3
(403) 233-2370

Family Court Services
811 14th St. NW
Calgary, Alta.
T2N 2A4
(403) 283-4406

Family Conciliation Service
Royal LePage Building
10130 103 St.
3rd Flr.
Edmonton, Alta.
T5J 3N9
(403) 427-8329

Lethbridge Family Services
515 7th St. S.
Lethbridge, Alta.
T1J 2G8
(403) 327-5724

British Columbia

Conciliation Services
The Law Courts
800 Smithe St.
Room 200
Vancouver, B.C.
V7Z 2E1
(604) 660-2694

Family Services of Greater Vancouver
1616 West 7th Ave.
Vancouver, B.C.
V6J 1S5
(604) 731-4951

Victoria Probation and Family Court Services
2020 Cameron St.
Victoria, B.C.
V8T 3N5
(604) 387-1896

Northwest Territories

Family Counselling Service
P.O. Box 1205
Yellowknife, N.W.T.
X1A 2N9
(403) 920-4846

PARENT SUPPORT GROUPS

The Joint Custody Association
10606 Wilkins Ave.
Los Angeles, Calif. 90024
(213) 475-5352

Contact the above address for listings of fathers- and mothers-without-custody groups in your province.

Parents Without Partners Inc. (Canada)
P.O. Box 1218, Stn. "B"
Oshawa, Ont.
L1J 5Z1
(416) 436-2255

One Parent Families Association of Canada
National Office
6979 Yonge St.
Ste. 203
Willowdale, Ont.
M2M 3X9
(416) 226-0062

OTHER ASSOCIATIONS

Canadian Association of Separated and Divorced Catholics
c/o Catholic Information Centre
830 Bathurst St.
Toronto, Ont.
M5R 3G1
(416) 534-2326

PROVINCIAL SOURCES FOR FAMILY LAW ACT
INFORMATION

Newfoundland

Department of Justice
Confederation Bldg.
St. John's, Nfld.
A1C 5T7
(709) 576-5942

Prince Edward Island

Department of Justice
Shaw Bldg.
73 Rochford St.
Box 2000
Charlottetown, P.E.I.
C1A 7N8
(902) 368-4550

Nova Scotia

Department of the Attorney General
Bank of Montreal Bldg.,
5151 George Street
10th Floor
Box 7
Halifax, N.S.
B3J 2L6
(902) 424-4222

New Brunswick

Department of Justice
Centennial Building
Box 6000
Fredericton, N.B.
E3B 5H1
(506) 453-2452

Quebec

Ministère de la justice
1200, rte. de l'Eglise
Ste-Foy, P.Q.
G1V 4M1
(418) 643-5140

Ontario

Ministry of the Attorney General
18 King St. E.
Toronto, Ont.
M5C 1C5
(416) 326-2200

Manitoba

Department of the Attorney General
405 Broadway Ave.
9th Flr.
Winnipeg, Man.
R3C 3L6
(204) 945-2211

Saskatchewan

Communications and Public Affairs
Department of Justice
1874 Scarth St.
Regina, Sask.
S4P 3V6
(306) 787-8971

Alberta

Department of the Attorney General
The Bowker Bldg.
9833-109 St.
Edmonton, Alta.
T5K 2E8
(403) 427-2745

British Columbia

Ministry of the Attorney General
Parliament Bldgs.
Victoria, B.C.
V8V 1X4
(604) 387-4577

Northwest Territories

Department of Justice
Building 163
Box 1030
Iqaluit, N.W.T.
X0A 0H0
(819) 979-5324

Yukon

Department of Justice
Financial Plaza
204 Lambert St.
Main Flr.
Whitehorse, Y.T.
Y1A 1Z4
(406) 668-7171

Selected Bibliography

* Books and articles on shared parenting

CHILD DEVELOPMENT

Bibby, Reginald W., and Donald C. Posterski. *The Emerging Generation: An Inside Look at Canada's Teenagers.* Toronto: Irwin Publishing, 1985.

Briggs, Dorothy Corkille. *Your Child's Self-Esteem.* Garden City, N.Y.: Dolphin Books, 1975.

Dreikurs, Rudolf. *Children: The Challenge.* New York: E.P. Dutton, 1964.

Leach, Penelope. *Your Baby and Child.* New York: Alfred A. Knopf, 1982.

DIVORCE

Ambert, Anne-Marie. *Divorce in Canada.* Toronto: Academic Press, 1980.

Berger, Stuart. *Divorce Without Victims.* Boston: Houghton Mifflin, 1983.

Demo, David H., and Alan C. Acock. "The Impact of Divorce on Children." *Journal of Marriage and the Family* 50 (1988).

Gerstel, Naomi. "Divorce and Stigma." *Social Problems* 34 (1987).

Hetherington, E. Mavis. "Divorce: A Child's Perspective." *American Psychologist* 34 (1979).

Johnson, Colleen Leahy. "Socially Controlled Civility: The Functioning of Rituals in the Divorce Process." *American Behavioral Scientist* 31 (1988).

Krantzler, Mel. *Creative Divorce*. New York: M. Evans and Co., 1973.

Lazrus, Arnold A. "Divorce Counseling or Marriage Therapy? A Therapeutic Option." *Journal of Marital and Family Therapy*, January 1981.

Wallerstein, Judith S., and Sandra Blakeslee. *Second Chances*. New York: Ticknor & Fields, 1989.

LAW

Batten, Jack, and Marjorie Harris. *Everyday Law: A Survival Guide for Canadians*. Toronto: A Lorraine Greey Book/Key Porter Books, 1987.

Boyd, Susan. "Child Custody Law Reinforces Women's Inequality." *Canadian Dimension* 23 (1989).

Department of Justice Canada. *Divorce Law for Counsellors*. Ottawa: Minister of Supply and Services Canada, 1989.

International Self-Counsel Press. *Divorce Guides*. North Vancouver, B.C., 1986.

Lipovenko, Dorothy. "Custody Rulings Curb Mothers' Mobility." *Globe and Mail*, October 17, 1989.

Takas, Marianne. *Child Custody*. New York: Harper & Row, 1987.

MEDIATION

Department of Justice Canada. *Another Way: Mediation in Divorce and Separation*. Ottawa: Minister of Supply and Services Canada, 1988.

Emery, Robert E., and Melissa M. Wyer. "Child Custody Mediation and Litigation." *Journal of Consulting and Clinical Psychology* 55 (1987).

Irving, Howard H., and Michael Benjamin. *Family Mediation: Theory and Practice of Dispute Resolution*. Toronto: Carswell, 1987.

PARENTING

*Adler, Robert E. *Sharing the Children*. Bethesda, Md.: Adler & Adler, 1988.

Aisenberg, Linda. "Two Moms Are Better Than One." *Chatelaine*, October 1987.

*Bienenfeld, Florence. *Helping Your Child Succeed After Divorce*. Claremont, Calif.: Hunter House, 1987.

Bishop, Sue Marquis, and Gary M. Ingersoll. "Effect of Marital Conflict and Family Structure on the Self-Concept of Pre- and Early Adolescents." *Journal of Youth and Adolescence* 18 (1989).

Brazelton, T. Berry. *Families: Crisis and Caring*. Reading, Mass.: Addison-Wesley Publishing, 1989.

Bustanoby, Andre. *Being a Single Parent*. New York: Ballantine Books, 1985.

Cole, Cynthia, and Hyman Rodman. "When School-Age Children Care for Themselves: Issues for Family Life Educators and Parents." *Family Relations*, January 1987.

Denham, Thomas E., and Craig W. Smith. "The Influence

of Grandparents on Grandchildren." *Family Relations*, October 1989.

Dodson, Fitzhugh. *How to Father*. Los Angeles: Nash Publishing, 1974.

*Elkin, Meyer. "Joint Custody: Affirming that Parents and Families Are Forever." *Social Work*, January/February 1987.

*Galper, Miriam. *Joint Custody and Co-Parenting*. Philadelphia, Pa.: Running Press, 1980.

Gardner, Richard A. *The Parents Book About Divorce*. Garden City, N.Y.: Doubleday, 1977.

Goldstein, Sol. *Divorced Parenting: How to Make It Work*. Toronto: McGraw-Hill Ryerson, 1982.

Gordon, Thomas. *P.E.T.: Parent Effectiveness Training*. New York: Peter H. Wyden, 1970.

*Hagen, Jan L. "Proceed with Caution: Advocating Joint Custody." *Social Work*, January/February 1987.

Kersey, Katharine. *Helping Your Child Handle Stress*. Washington, D.C.: Acropolis Books, 1986.

_____. *Sensitive Parenting from Infancy to Adulthood*. Washington, D.C.: Acropolis Books, 1983.

*Kline, Marsha, et al. "Children's Adjustment in Joint and Sole Physical Custody Families." *Developmental Psychology* 25 (1989).

Lansky, Vicki. *Vicki Lansky's Divorce Book for Parents*. New York: NAL Books, 1989.

*McKinnon, Rosemary, and Judith Wallerstein. "A Preventive Intervention Program for Parents and Young Children in Joint Custody Arrangements." *American Journal of Orthopsychiatry* 58 (1988).

*Morgenbesser, Mel, and Nadine Nehls. *Joint Custody: An Alternative for Divorcing Families*. Chicago: Nelson-Hall, 1981.

*Pitkeathly, Doreen. "Who Gets the Kids?" *Canadian Living*, September 5, 1987.

Rossiter, Amy Burdick. "A Model for Group Intervention with Preschool Children Experiencing Separation and Divorce." *American Journal of Orthopsychiatry* 58 (1988).

Rejnis, Ruth. *The Single Parent's Housing Guide*. New York: M.Evans and Co., 1984.

*Ricci, Isolina. *Mom's House, Dad's House*. New York: Collier Books, 1980.

Rich, Dorothy. *MegaSkills: How Families Can Help Children Succeed in School and Beyond*. Boston: Houghton Mifflin, 1988.

Roseman, Ellen, and Colleen Darragh. *The Canadian Parents' Sourcebook*. Toronto: Doubleday, 1986.

Rosenstock, Janet and Eva M. Rosenstock. *Child Care: Options for Working Parents*. Toronto: Methuen, 1985.

Teyber, Edward. *Helping Your Children with Divorce*. New York: Pocket Books, 1985.

*Ware, Ciji. *Sharing Parenthood After Divorce*. New York: The Viking Press, 1982.

Wayman, Anne. *Successful Single Parenting*. New York: Meadowbrook, 1987.

*Zemmelman, Steven E., et al. "A Model Project on Joint Custody for Families Undergoing Divorce." *Social Work*, January/February, 1987.

STEPPARENTING

Berman, Claire. *Making It as a Stepparent*. New York: Harper & Row, 1986.

Clubb, Angela Neumann. *Love in the Blended Family*. Toronto: NC Press, 1988.

Paris, Erna. *Stepfamilies: Making Them Work*. New York: Avon Books, 1984.

Visher, Emily B., and John S. Visher. *Stepfamilies: Myths and Realities*. Secaucus, N.J.: The Citadel Press, 1979.

BOOK LIST FOR CHILDREN

For Younger Children

Brown, Laurene Krasny. *Dinosaurs Divorce: A Guide for Changing Families*. Boston: Atlantic Monthly Press, 1986.

Christiansen, C.B. *My Mother's House, My Father's House*. New York: Atheneum/Collier Macmillan, 1989.

Hazen, Barbara Shook. *Two Homes to Live In: A Child's-Eye View of Divorce*. New York: Human Sciences Press, 1983.

Stinson, Kathy. *Mom and Dad Don't Live Together Anymore*. Toronto: Annick Press, 1984.

For Older Children

Blume, Judy. *It's Not the End of the World*. Scarsdale, N.Y.: Bradbury Press, 1972.

Danziger, Paula. *The Divorce Express*. New York: Delacorte Press, 1982.

Department of the Attorney General, Ontario. *Where Do*

I Stand? A Child's Legal Guide to Separation and Divorce. Toronto: Department of the Attorney General, 1986.

Gardner, Richard. *The Boys' and Girls' Book About Divorce*. Toronto: Bantam, 1970.

Krementz, Jill. *How It Feels When Parents Divorce*. New York: Knopf, 1984.

Major, Kevin. *Dear Bruce Springsteen: A Novel*. Toronto: Doubleday, 1987.

Richards, Arlene. *How to Get It Together When Your Parents Are Coming Apart*. New York: D. McKay, 1976.

Robson, Bonnie. *My Parents Are Divorced, Too*. Toronto: Dorset, 1979.

BOOK LIST FOR GRANDPARENTS
Gottlieb, Dorothy Weiss, et al. *What to Do When Your Son or Daughter Divorces*. New York: Bantam Books, 1988.

FILMS
National Film Board. *Dad's House, Mom's House*. 1985.

Index